POCKET-PEDIA

1001+ FANTASTIC FACTS *about* SCIENCE

DAN GREEN

BARRON'S

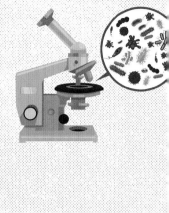
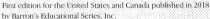

First edition for the United States and Canada published in 2018
by Barron's Educational Series, Inc.

First published in Great Britain in 2017 by Arcturus Publishing Limited
26/27 Bickels Yard, 151-153 Bermondsey Street
London SE1 3HA

Author: Dan Green
Designer: Amy McSimpson @ Hollow Pond
Editors: Clare Hibbert @ Hollow Pond and Joe Harris
Illustrator: Jake McDonald
Supplementary Artwork: Shutterstock
Science Consultant: Thomas Canavan

All inquiries should be addressed to:
Barron's Educational Series, Inc.
250 Wireless Boulevard
Hauppauge, New York 11788
www.barronseduc.com

ISBN: 978-1-4380-1193-6
Library of Congress Control Number: 2017958538
Date of Manufacture: May 2018
Manufactured by: 1010 Printing, Hui Zhou City, China

Printed in China

9 8 7 6 5 4 3 2 1

CONTENTS

ALL LIFE ON EARTH
USES THE SAME BASIC PROGRAMMING
The programming language is DNA!

chromosome

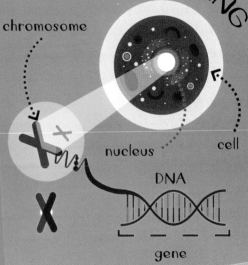

nucleus

cell

DNA

gene

DYNAMIC DNA

DNA is a molecule shaped like a long, twisty ladder. It is found in the nucleus at the middle of each of your body's cells. Like computer code, it holds instructions, called genes. This chemical code keeps you alive and helps you grow. Long chains of genes are called chromosomes.

COPYCATS

They may not look it, but all living things on Earth are amazingly similar in the way they are built. All living things have DNA in their cells, and much of the basic genetic code that runs their bodies is the same.

ALL LIFE ON EARTH IS KEPT GOING BY
ONE CHEMICAL REACTION

Green plants keep themselves—and everything else—alive by capturing energy from the Sun.

LIFEGIVER

The Sun is the source of all the energy that keeps life on our planet going. Plants use a chemical reaction called **photosynthesis** to take energy from sunlight. So do other creatures, such as plankton.

GRUB'S UP!

Plants use captured sunlight to create sugary food and build their cells. Other living things eat plants to get energy, and then meat-eaters chow down on the "vegetarians!"

Sunlight-using living things are called **producers**. They make their own food.

5

We hardly know anything about
EARTH'S MOST COMMON CREATURES

The planet belongs to bacteria, smaller than the eye can see.

A drop of seawater can contain a million bacteria.

CELL—SATIONAL!

Made up of just a single cell, **bacteria** are the simplest living creatures on the planet. Beastly bacteria cause disease, spoil food, and rot our teeth. But they also pump breathable oxygen into the air, help us digest our food, help plants to grow, and break down waste matter.

MIGHTY MICROBES

There are a 100 million times more bacteria in the sea than there are stars in the Universe. Yet, we know little about most of them.

SOME LIVING THINGS CAN SURVIVE IN BATTERY ACID

Acid-loving microbes live in hot springs, polluted mines—and your stomach!

hot spring

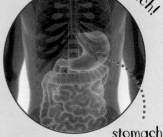

stomach

Pollution from a mine.

HOT BATH

Picrophilus holds the record for coping with acid. It even survives quite happily in 140-°F (60-°C) water, which can be more caustic (burning) than sulfuric acid.

EXTREME LIFE

Some bacteria can thrive in very harsh conditions. These extreme organisms live in deadly hot and cold temperatures, soak up salt, dangerous radiation, and even bathe happily in acid. Scientists think they would have been tough enough to cope with conditions when Earth was young and may have been some of the first lifeforms on the planet.

LIFE BEGAN IN DEEP-SEA VENTS

In 1977, scientists found life at the bottom of the ocean, far beyond the Sun's reach.

Bacteria have been around for at least 3.5 billion years.

DEEP QUESTION

One of the great questions is how life began on our planet. When scientists discovered a thriving community of **organisms** (living things) near deep-sea vents, some of them wondered if life might have started here, far from the light of the Sun. It is thought that bacteria live off the chemical soup around the vents and that larger organisms, such as tubeworms, then feed on them.

STARTING OUT

All the raw materials to build life are found at deep-sea vents. Early organisms would also have been safe from the Sun's damaging radiation.

THOUSANDS OF NEW SPECIES ARE DISCOVERED EVERY YEAR

About half of them are insects!

land

14% known

86% yet to be found

9% known

sea

91% yet to be found

CREATURE HUNT

Scientists think that there is space on the planet for 8.74 million different species, but around 7 million of these are yet to be discovered! More than 15,000 new species are found each year.

Old and new

Not all new species are found in the wild. Many are found in museum collections. In 2016, a new species of meat-eating plant was identified in a picture on Facebook.

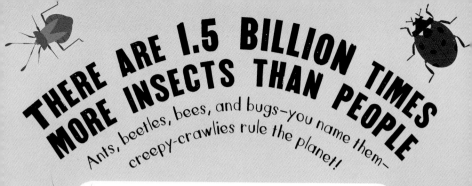

THERE ARE 1.5 BILLION TIMES MORE INSECTS THAN PEOPLE

Ants, beetles, bees, and bugs—you name them—creepy-crawlies rule the planet!

INSECTS RULE!

The six-legged creatures we call insects are the world's most successful animals. An estimated 10 quintillion (10,000,000,000,000,000,000) insects are alive today. There is no shortage of beetles. Line up all the animals and plants in a row and every fifth one would be a beetle.

For every person living on Earth there are about 1.4 million ants!

HEAVYWEIGHT HERO

The giant **weta** is the world's heaviest insect. This scale-busting, 2.5-oz (70-g) bruiser is three times heavier than a mouse.

A FLEA ACCELERATES FASTER THAN A SPACE ROCKET

These tiny, bloodsucking bugs have super-powered legs!

FIT AS A FLEA

These tiny biting beasties take off so fast they have to withstand 100 Gs—that's 100 times the force of gravity. The average g-force experienced by astronauts on board space rockets is around 3 Gs.

A flea clears 38 times its own body length. That's the same as a human hopping over four buses in a single jump.

LEAP LIKE A FLEA

Time taken for a flea spring:
1/1000 second

Jump speed:
6.2 ft (1.9 m)/second

Average leap length:
3 in (7.6 cm)

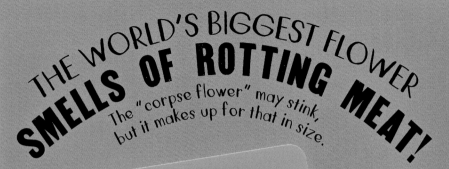

THE WORLD'S BIGGEST FLOWER
SMELLS OF ROTTING MEAT!

The "corpse flower" may stink, but it makes up for that in size.

MEGAFLOWER

The **titan arum** has a truly strange flower. Towering 10 ft (3 m) high, it looks like a wrinkled finger sticking out of a paper cupcake case. Strictly speaking, it is many flowers attached to one tall stalk.

WHY SO STINKY?

The smell of rotting meat would be unpleasant to us, but it attracts dung beetles and flesh flies in droves. They carry the titan arum's pollen!

CABBAGES, BRUSSELS SPROUTS, AND CAULIFLOWERS
ARE THE SAME PLANT

Discover the hidden secrets of the world's most versatile vegetable.

Broccoli has bulbous flower heads

Cauliflower has super-specialized flower heads

THE SAME DIFFERENCE

Meet the humble wild mustard plant, *Brassica oleracea*. Over hundreds of years, farmers have cultivated plants of this single species to create more than a half a dozen different versions.

Kale plants have bigger leaves

Cabbages have tightly packed leaves

Kohlrabi plants have thick stalks

Brussels sprouts have leafy buds along the stem

13

Ninety-five percent of plant foods
COME FROM JUST 30 CROPS

The staple diet of humans is surprisingly limited!

rice

PERILOUS POSITION

Humankind has cultivated crops that provide the highest output for the smallest area. As well as being quite boring, this tactic makes our food supplies vulnerable to climate change.

EAT YOUR GREENS!

Plants make up more than four-fifths of our diet, yet we only eat about 30 different species. Nearly two-thirds of our food energy requirements are provided by just five crops—rice, wheat, maize, millet, and sorghum.

wheat

corn

BRANCH OUT

If you're in the mood for trying something different, there are as many as 30,000 different species of edible plants to try.

SEVENTY THOUSAND
PLANT SPECIES ARE USED FOR MEDICINE

All kinds of plants are used to make cures
for diseases or to relieve ailments.

Roots, shoots, and leaves

Herbal remedies are made directly from plant
extracts. These natural treatments tend to be
traditional medicines used to
treat everyday sicknesses,
such as peppermint
leaves to soothe an
upset stomach.

peppermint
tea

About a
quarter of the
ingredients in
modern medicines
come from rain
forest plants.

AMAZING MEDICINES

Modern medicines are **inorganic** (not living)
chemicals made in a lab. Many of them are
copied from nature. The headache drug
aspirin contains an active ingredient first
found in the bark of the willow tree.

15

RAIN FOREST LIFE

A **rain forest** is a place where at least 98 in (250 cm) of rain falls in a year, but some get double that amount.

The mighty Amazon rain forest produces one-fifth of Earth's oxygen.

The Amazon rain forest is the biggest tropical rain forest in the world.

An area of tropical rain forest greater than 45,000 football fields is destroyed every day.

There are 400 billion trees in the Amazon rain forest.

The tropical rain forests of Latin America are home to the loudest primate, the howler monkey, whose call can be heard over 3 miles (5 km) away!

Not even one percent of rain forest plants have been studied for use as medicine.

Rain forests cover just 6 percent of the planet's surface, but contain half of the world's species.

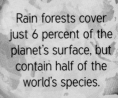

A huge number of products come from rain forests—bananas, avocados, Brazil nuts, coffee, palm oil, cocoa, and vanilla, not to mention tropical hardwoods.

Giant bamboo shoots grow up to 9 in (22 cm) a day.

17

NOT ALL RAIN FORESTS ARE TROPICAL

The world's biggest and most famous rain forests are in the tropics, but colder regions have soggy woodlands, too.

RAIN, RAIN GO AWAY!

There are two types of rain forests—**tropical** and **temperate**. Both are wet, but temperate rain forests are only hot during the summer months. In winter, it's cold. This means that different kinds of trees grow there.

In the clouds

Cloud forests grow high up on mountainsides. Wrapped in permanent clouds, the fog drips constantly. Although always cold, due to their altitude, these mossy rain forests can be found in both tropical and temperate regions.

THE WORLD'S LARGEST

LIVING THING IS A MUSHROOM

Blue whales have nothing on a giant American parasitic fungus.

HUMUNGOUS FUNGUS

The largest living thing on the planet is a honey fungus. Living in the Blue Mountains of Oregon, it is 2.4 miles (3.8 km) wide! When this branching beast meets up with genetically identical mushrooms, they merge together.

The yellow-brown mushrooms that pop up above ground are just the tip of this fungus iceberg. Most of the organism lives underground, in a spreading network of strings and tubes.

THE CALIFORNIA REDWOOD IS
THE TALLEST LIVING THING
Northern California is home to the world's most tremendous trees.

REACH FOR THE SKY

The world's tallest tree is a lanky lunk of lumber called Hyperion. It's 379.7 ft (115.7 m) tall—that's 70 ft (21 m) taller than the Statue of Liberty!

GIANT GIRTH

Redwoods measure 24 ft (7 m) around their base. Giant sequoias are not as tall, but have much thicker trunks. "General Sherman" is 275 ft (84 m) tall, and measures a giant 102 ft (31 m) around its base.

JUMBO TRUNKS

Hyperion weighs an estimated 1.6 million lbs (725,700 kg)—that's more than three blue whales.

MOST TREES ARE 99 PERCENT DEAD

The largest part of a tree's woody body is not its living cells.

GREEN SHOOTS

Although a tree is a living thing, not all of its cells actively do the sorts of things living cells do, namely, changing chemicals. In a fully grown tree, living cells are only found in the growing portions—leaves, buds, roots, and a thin skin of cells under the bark.

DEAD, BUT NOT USELESS

A sapling is supercharged—all its cells are frantically growing. A mature tree is much calmer. Tough, woody cells help it to stand upright, while the outer bark protects the soft living cells underneath.

21

GINGKOS
HAVE BEEN AROUND FOR MILLIONS OF YEARS
Dinosaurs roamed through gingko forests!

LIVING FOSSIL

Gingkos have remained largely unchanged for over 200 million years. Fossilized leaf imprints of this tree turn up in sedimentary rocks from the Permian Period, not long before the Age of the Dinosaurs. Gingkos today are a species with no living relatives.

Gingko berries smell of vomit!

Rough and tough relic
Surviving for this long, it's no surprise that the gingko is tough. This tree often lines city streets.

THE OLDEST LIVING THING IS THE BRISTLECONE PINE

The longest-lived organism on the planet was already a youngster by the time the Ancient Egyptians started building pyramids.

TOP THREE OLD-TIMERS

Sacred fig tree
Country: Sri Lanka
Age: At least 2,222 years old

Patagonian cypress tree
Country: Chile
Age: 3,627 years old

Great Basin bristlecone pine
Country: USA
Age: 5,067 years old

TOP SECRET

The location of the oldest bristlecone pine is a well-kept secret, to stop it from becoming a tourist attraction.

23

SOME ANIMALS LIVE FOR CENTURIES

The record for the oldest living thing goes to a clam called the ocean quahog.

MEET "MING"

The **quahog** lives in the North Atlantic and grows to around 2 in (5 cm) across. No one knows exactly how long it can live, but one individual—called Ming—lived for 507 years!

A tortoise called Tu'i Malila lived to the age of 189. Other tortoises may have lived longer!

✓ Red sea urchins can live for more than 200 years.

✓ Bowhead whales live for more than 200 years.

✓ One Greenland shark was known to have lived for more than 400 years.

The Great Barrier Reef is the
LARGEST LIVING STRUCTURE
MADE BY LIVING THINGS

Australia's Great Barrier Reef covers an area larger than Italy. It is so big, it can be seen from space.

SEALIFE PARADISE

Australia's Great Barrier Reef is one of Earth's natural wonders. Stretching 1,429 miles (2,300 km) down the northeastern coast, the Great Barrier Reef contains over 3,000 individual reefs, and is home to around one in ten of the world's marine fish species.

The reef is under threat from "coral bleaching," which happens when the living parts of the corals lose their bright shades and die away.

LIFE OF THE OCEANS

Nearly three-quarters of Earth's surface is covered by oceans.

Plankton in the ocean provide most of the oxygen in our atmosphere.

As the Moon orbits Earth, its gravity pulls seawater toward it, making two tides every day.

All five major oceans are connected to each other. The Pacific Ocean is the largest.

Waves are created by winds blowing across the water.

The Bay of Fundy in Newfoundland has the world's highest tides. They have a sea-level rise and fall of 53.5 ft (16.3 m).

The world's longest mountain range stretches 40,389 miles (65,000 km), through the middle of the oceans.

The name of the Pacific Ocean is taken from Latin, and means "peaceful."

There are about 22 million tons (20 million tonnes) of gold dissolved in the oceans.

Possibly as many as 3 million shipwrecks litter the ocean floors.

NEARLY ALL LIVING THINGS ON
EARTH ARE IN THE OCEANS

Life started out in the oceans, and most of it stayed there!

WONDERFUL LIFE

Scientists say that 99 percent of the living space on Earth is in the seas. So it's no surprise to learn that 94 percent of organisms live there. What is surprising, though, is that we have only met a fraction of them.

HERE'S LOOKING AT YOU

The biggest eyes in the world belong to the colossal squid. This sea monster's eyes grow to the size of a human head!

Seahorses are the only animal in which the male becomes pregnant.

THE SEA CAN GLOW

Ancient sailors called it "the burning of the sea"—eerie blue lights that appear on dark nights where seawater is disturbed.

BIZARRE BIOLUMINESCENCE

Many sea creatures create light, but microscopic plankton produce the weirdest effect. Tiny neon pinpricks of light look like a floating field of stars. Scientists think these light signals act like a burglar alarm, alerting big animals to the presence of the plankton's predators. Larger predators arrive to feed on the plankton's enemies.

More than four in five ocean animals have the ability to produce light.

The scientific word for glowing creatures is **bioluminescence** (say bye-oh-loom-min-ess-ents).

THE OCEAN'S DEADLIEST ANIMAL IS THE BLUE-RINGED OCTOPUS

A cute little eight-legged beast, decorated with bright electric-blue rings, is one of the most toxic creatures on Earth!

TINY TERROR

Barely bigger than a stubby pencil from head to tentacle tip, the blue-ringed octopus has one of the most powerful known venoms. A nip from its sharp beak causes numbness of the lips, followed by violent vomiting. The affected muscles make even sitting difficult, breathing becomes impossible, and death follows within six hours . . . unless you find help!

WARNING SIGNS

If disturbed, the octopus flashes the neon blue warning circles on its body and legs. Better clear out!

The fastest animal in the sea
IS THE BLACK MARLIN

Organizing speed trials for fish is tricky to say the least. Usually, a fish's speed is measured by the rate at which it pulls the line from a fisherman's reel. However, this measurement is complicated by the speed of the boat and the direction of water currents.

WORLD'S FASTEST FISH

The black marlin is the speed champ of the seas, having been recorded unreeling a fishing line at 80 mph (129 kph).

SUPER SWIMMERS

All fish have streamlined bodies, but black marlin have bullet-shaped bodies and sharp bills to cut through the water. Curved tail fins give them turbo-charged acceleration, too.

SALTY ICICLES FORM IN VERY COLD WATER

Strange fingers of death called "brinicles" creep down through freezing water in the Arctic and Antarctic, killing everything in their path. This is how it happens:

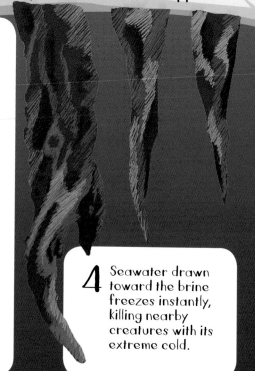

1 Polar air temperatures hover around -4 °F (-20 °C), but seawater is -28.58 °F (-1.9 °C). Heat moves from the warmer water to the air. Sea ice forms at the surface.

2 Salt is excluded as ice crystals form. Salt-heavy brine builds up in cracks and channels within the sea ice.

3 The concentrated brine sinks. It is now below the freezing point of seawater, since salt-rich water freezes at lower temperatures.

4 Seawater drawn toward the brine freezes instantly, killing nearby creatures with its extreme cold.

THE OCEAN IS FULL OF STRANGE SOUNDS

Dip a hydrophone (underwater microphone) into the water to hear the seas' spookiest sounds.

UNIDENTIFIED OCEAN SOUNDS

Mystery sounds in the ocean are given unusual names. "The Bloop" was a powerful, ultra-low-frequency sound, picked up in 1997 by listening stations thousands of miles apart. It may have been caused by an underwater icequake, a volcanic eruption, or an iceberg, but if the source was an animal, it would be bigger than a blue whale.

UNDERSEA SONG

The blue whale's song is the loudest sound made by an animal. Its 188-decibels solo effort can be heard 500 miles (800 km) away.

33

THE DEEP, DEEP SEA

Mount Everest

The ocean is 2.3 miles (3.7 km) deep on average. That's about eight Empire State Buildings, stacked on top of each other.

The deepest point in the ocean is the Mariana Trench, about 190 miles (300 km) southwest of Guam in the Pacific Ocean.

Mount Everest would comfortably fit into the Mariana Trench, with a mile or so to spare.

Challenger Deep, part of the Mariana Trench, is 36,200 ft (11,030 m) deep. That's the height of 25 stacked Empire State Buildings.

Giant squid can grow as long as a double-decker bus.

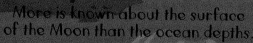

More is known about the surface of the Moon than the ocean depths.

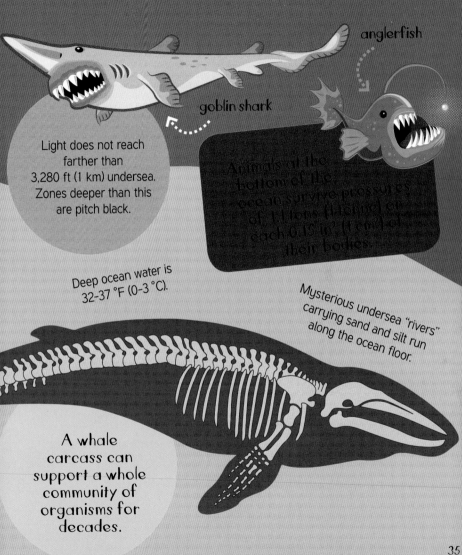

anglerfish

goblin shark

Light does not reach farther than 3,280 ft (1 km) undersea. Zones deeper than this are pitch black.

Animals at the bottom of the ocean survive pressures of 1.1 tons (1 tonne) on each 0.15 in² (1 cm²) of their bodies.

Deep ocean water is 32-37 °F (0-3 °C).

Mysterious undersea "rivers" carrying sand and silt run along the ocean floor.

A whale carcass can support a whole community of organisms for decades.

THE LARGEST PREDATOR THAT EVER LIVED
WASN'T A DINOSAUR
Giant Liopleurodon was a prehistoric sea monster.

BIG HEAD

Liopleurodon was a giant sea reptile that lived at the same time as the dinosaurs. Snaggle-toothed and short-necked, it used its strong flippers to power it swiftly through the water. Like today's sharks, Liopleurodon was an apex predator, with no natural predators of its own.

LIOPLEURODON FACTFILE

Say: LY-oh-PLUH-roh-don

Size: 16-23 ft (5-7 m) long

Diet: Fish and other marine reptiles

Lived: Mid to Late Jurassic, 160-155 million years ago

Liopleurodon's 18-in (46-cm) teeth were longer than a bread knife.

One prehistoric shark had
TEETH LIKE A CHAINSAW

The world's oddest sea creature lived in the Permian period, 270 million years ago.

BUZZSAW JAW

Weird and wild-looking, **Helicoprion** is an extinct ratfish with a tightly curled coil of teeth at the front of its mouth. Dino scientists think that this bristling wheel o' tooth was attached to the fish's bottom jaw, but no one really knows how it used the thing!

Squid dish

Helicoprion's backward-pointing vertical tooth wheel may have been perfect for slicing through soft mollusks, such as octopuses and squid.

Helicoprion (say HEH-lih-COPE-ree-on) is Greek for "spiral saw."

CHALK IS MADE FROM
TRILLIONS OF MICROFOSSILS

The famous, towering white cliffs of England, France, and Denmark are made from mini fossils smaller than the eye can see!

Most chalk was laid down in the Cretaceous period, between 100 and 60 million years ago.

MUDDY END

Chalk was once a fine mud on the seabed. This gungy ooze was made from the microscopic remains of tiny plankton that had sunk to the bottom when they died.

HERE ARE SOME OF THE MICROFOSSILS YOU CAN FIND IN CHALK:

Forams
Ostracods
Diatoms
Dinoflagellates
Coccoliths
Radiolarians

THE LARGEST FLYING INSECT EVER HAD A BIRD-SIZED WINGSPAN

Lucky for us, this prehistoric pest lived 300 million years ago!

Meganeura

GIANT DRAGONFLY

Less fly and more dragon, **Meganeura** measured around 26 in (65 cm) from wingtip to wingtip. That's roughly the same as a pigeon! Like today's dragonflies, Meganeura laid its eggs in water and probably spent most of its life as a larva in the water.

Supercharged insects

High oxygen levels in the Carboniferous period boosted insect sizes. Some of the fearsome frights that lived at the time include a millipede that was 7.5 ft (2.3 m) long—longer than a king-sized bed!

Stegosaurus' brain was
NO BIGGER THAN A WALNUT

Stegosaurus may have had giant tail-spikes,
but it didn't have a giant brain!

DOPEY DINO?

Many dinosaurs had small brains, because much of
the space in their skulls was used to anchor powerful
biting muscles. Although its brain was the same size as
a walnut, it was shaped more like a sausage.

brain

walnut

Stegosaurus
means "roofed
lizard," because
paleontologists'
first thought the
dino's plates were
like roofing tiles.

Stegosaurus
lived during
the late Jurassic
Period, about
155-150 million
years ago.

THE ANCESTOR OF ALL VERTEBRATES WAS A WORMLIKE CREATURE

Vertebrates are animals with backbones. This group includes fish, amphibians, reptiles, mammals, and birds.

SWIMMING WRIGGLERS

Animals with backbones evolved in the sea during the Cambrian period, about 500 million years ago. The first vertebrates looked like worms. These mini-wrigglers, smaller than a paper clip, swam free in the ancient oceans. They may not look much like us, but just like all animals with backbones, these Cambrian critters have top-to-bottom symmetrical bodies and blocks of muscles attached to the spine to move them about.

Myllokunmingia

Cathaymyrus

One modern creature looks remarkably similar to these ancient ancestors. The **lancelet** lives half-buried in sand on riverbeds.

ARE DINOSAURS EXTINCT?

You may think dinosaurs died out 65 million years ago. But their descendants are possibly still with us. We just call them birds!

Tyrannosaurus rex

DINO BIRDS

The prehistoric monsters we know from blockbuster movies may be gone for good . . . but birds are alive and well. Birds are the direct relatives of the dinosaurs. While the big brutes died out after a huge asteroid hit Earth 65 million years ago, smaller, fast-moving birds survived.

magpie

heron

Utahraptor

TWEETYSAURUS

You can easily spot the birdy in a dinosaur. From T. rex to Archaeopteryx, they had wishbones. Their pelvis bones pointed backward like a bird's and some dinosaurs also had feathers, although most were too heavy to use them to fly.

crested caracara   Velociraptor

A SMILODON'S TEETH
WERE HUGE, BUT QUITE WEAK

The teeth of these prehistoric saber-toothed cats look fearsome, but they were tricky to use.

Smilodon was a mammal who lived about 2 million years ago. Modern-day big cats clamp their jaws around the necks of their prey to suffocate it. Smilodon's jaw muscles weren't strong enough for that. Instead, they used their powerful forelegs to bring down buffaloes, horses, or giant ground sloths. Then they used their huge teeth to deliver a quick and fatal stab to the throat.

The saber-toothed cat's dagger-like teeth measured 8 in (20 cm) long.

OPEN WIDE!

To get any food past its enormous front teeth, Smilodon had to open its mouth very wide.

ICE AGE LIFE

There have been at least five significant ice ages in Earth's history

During the most recent Ice Age, snow and ice permanently covered huge parts of the planet.

The last Ice Age lasted about 100,000 years, between 110,000 to 12,000 years ago.

A woolly mammoth's tusks were about 8.9 ft (2.7 m) long and weighed about 99 lbs (45 kg)—that's as heavy as four gold bars!

The largest land mammal that ever existed, Paraceratherium, was a 22-ton (20-tonne) giant, hornless rhino.

woolly mammoth

Large animals hold their body heat better than smaller ones, and fare better during cold periods.

Dire wolves were huge wolves. Their shaggy bodies were found trapped in tar pits in California.

Many woolly mammoth bodies have been found intact, buried in permafrost.

Scientists aim to bring mammoths back to life by putting their frozen DNA into elephant embryos.

One furry Ice Age rhino had a wide, flat horn for shovelling snow.

Many enormous animals lived during the Ice Age. They are known as **megafauna**.

Titanis

Megacerops

HUMANS DID NOT
EVOLVE FROM CHIMPS
But our family trees have a lot in common!

BALDER AND SMARTER

Humans are apes—just like chimpanzees. Our bodies share many similarities with them, because we share a common ancestor. It lived about three million years ago, and was neither a modern human nor a modern chimpanzee. We both evolved from this long-armed, small-brained, and hairy ancestor, but humans became short-armed, big-brained, and hairless creatures.

orangutan

gorilla

chimpanzee

human

GREAT APES

An incredible 98.8 percent of the DNA in humans and chimps is the same.

HUMANS HAVE SUPERSIZED BRAINS

They are unusually large for our body size.

HUMAN Number of brain cells: 16.3 billion

BIGGER BRAINS

Around 2.5 million years ago, our ancestors' brains got bigger. Fossils show that the brains of these early humans went from 20 fl oz (0.6 l—about two soft drink cans) to about 2 pints (1 l). This gave early humans a boost in intelligence.

Size isn't everything

Intelligence isn't *just* about big brains. Elephants and whales have much bigger brains than humans, but we have many more brain cells in the thinking parts of our brains.

ELEPHANT Number of brain cells: 5.59 billion

YOU MAY BE
PART-NEANDERTHAL

60,000 years ago, there were three human species—
Neanderthals, Denisovans, and modern humans. Today,
there is only one left: Homo sapiens. But many of us
carry genes from our big-boned, square-jawed, and
brawny cousins, the Neanderthals!

How can you tell if you are part-Neanderthal? *

Long skull

Brow ridge

Rosy cheeks

Bumpy knot of bone
at back of head

Big nose

ANCIENT ANCESTORS

Europeans and Asians
have between one
and four percent
Neanderthal
DNA. Africans
have none.

*The only
way of knowing
if you have
Neanderthal
DNA is to have
a DNA test.

THE LONGEST HUMAN LIFE LASTED 122 YEARS

On average, humans live to be 71 and a half years old, but some people knock this average out of the park!

OLDEST HUMAN EVER

Jeanne Calment had the longest human life ever recorded. The French supercentenarian was born in 1875 and died in 1997, aged 122 years and 164 days.

AGING COUNTRIES

With people living longer and fewer babies being born, some nations are actually getting older. In Japan, the number of people aged 60+ has quadrupled in the last 40 years.

THERE ARE OVER SEVEN BILLION
PEOPLE ON THE PLANET

Just over 100 years ago,
there were only one billion people living on
the planet. Today there are nearly 7.6 billion humans
alive, and by 2024, the world's population will hit 8 billion.

THIS IS WHERE MOST PEOPLE ON EARTH LIVE*:

Africa (17%)

Europe (10%)

Latin America and the Caribbean

Asia (60%)

(6%)

Northern America and Oceania

BIG POPULATIONS

The country with the most
people is China. About 1.4
billion people live there. India
is next, with 1.3 billion people.

*The numbers in this chart add up to more
than 100% because of rounding.

50

THERE ARE MORE KIDS ON EARTH THAN EVER BEFORE

There are 1.8 billion young people in the world aged between 10 and 24.

YOUTHQUAKE

Compared to 60 years ago, women have many fewer children. However, those babies are much more likely to survive to become adults. This means the world's population is still growing!

Niger in Africa has the youngest population in the world.

250 babies are born every minute.

All the humans on the planet COULD SQUEEZE INTO ONE CITY

Los Angeles

A SQUASH AND A SQUEEZE

The entire world's population could fit within the American city of Los Angeles. Imagine—7.6 billion people squeezed into just 500 mi^2 (1,300 km^2). There would be no way you could see the sights!

ONE STEP BEYOND

Why stop there? The atoms of our bodies are mostly empty space. If you could find a way to extract it and squeeze a person into the smallest possible volume . . . the whole human race would fit into a space the size of a sugar cube!

OVER HALF THE PEOPLE ON THE PLANET LIVE IN CITIES

10 of the world's top 20 fastest-growing cities are in China.

MEGA CITIES

Cities occupy a tiny amount of the available land on Earth. However, more than half of us live in one. One out of every five people lives in a large city with a population greater than 1 million. There are more than 30 mega cities, with over 10 million people.

Tokyo-Yokohama, Japan, is the largest urban area in the world. It is home to over 37 million people.

Macau in China is the most crowded city in the world, with nearly 53,000 people/mi² (20,500 people/km²).

Tokyo

53

OUR SOLAR SYSTEM IS 4.6 BILLION YEARS OLD

The Sun and the planets orbiting it are unimaginably old. Scientists think that they were created when a nearby star exploded.

HOW TO MAKE A SOLAR SYSTEM

1 Take a dust cloud floating in space and set off a massive explosion close by (an exploding star does the trick).

2 The cloud collapses in on itself and gets more and more dense.

3 When enough stuff is squeezed together in the middle, nuclear fusion reactions begin and a new star is born.

4 The new star is surrounded by a flat, spinning disk of leftover debris. Planets form out of this material to create a solar system!

MOST OF OUR SOLAR SYSTEM
IS IN THE SUN

Almost all of the solar system's mass is found in the huge star in the middle.

The Sun is really big, amazingly so. More than a million Earths could fit inside our star.

1 Sun
2 Mercury
3 Venus
4 Earth
5 Mars
6 Jupiter
7 Saturn
8 Uranus
9 Neptune

(Not drawn to scale)

LEFTOVERS

Our Sun contains 99.86 percent of all matter in our solar system. Everything else—all the planets and moons, as well as the countless asteroids, comets, and other amazing objects in our solar system—is made from the 0.14 percent left.

GIANT JUPITER

Most of the material that makes up that tiny 0.14 percent of leftovers is in Jupiter. Together with Saturn, it makes up more than 90 percent of the mass of all the planets.

ALL OUR SOLAR SYSTEM'S PLANETS TRAVEL IN THE SAME DIRECTION

Seen from "below" the solar system, all the planets move clockwise.

IN A SPIN

It might seem unlikely that all the planets would travel around the Sun in the same direction, but they do. They also orbit in the same plane, as if they were all spinning on a giant disk with the Sun in the middle. It all comes down to the way the solar system formed. As the cloud of dust and gas was pulled inward by its own gravity, it started to spin—like an ice skater does when she draws in her arms to spin faster.

IN JUST 2 BILLION YEARS,
EARTH'S OCEANS WILL EVAPORATE

It's just one effect of our star getting older.

THIS IS YOUR LIFE

The life span of a star like our Sun is about 10 billion years. This means that it is already about halfway through its life.

HEATING UP

As the Sun's core runs out of hydrogen, it will start burning up heavier fuel, growing brighter and hotter as a result. Two billion years from now, the Earth will be so hot that the water in our oceans will boil away. This will be the end of life on Earth and our planet will become a desert world, similar to Mars today.

MERCURY IS THE FASTEST PLANET

By the time Earth has looped around the Sun once, speedy Mercury has whizzed around it more than four times!

WHY SO FAST?

Mercury is the closest planet to the Sun, so its journey around the Sun is the shortest. This tiny, rocky planet is also held more tightly by the Sun's powerful gravity. It has to travel faster to balance the pull from the Sun.

SPEEDY MERCURY FACTS

* Mercury's average speed is 106,000 mph (170,505 kph).
* Mercury circles the Sun in just 88 Earth-days.

VENUS
IS THE HOTTEST PLANET

Venus is nearly twice as far from the Sun as Mercury, but it is actually hotter.

SISTER ACT

Venus is sometimes called our "sister planet" because it is almost exactly the same size as Earth. But the similarity ends there! Venus has a dense atmosphere of carbon dioxide. Clouds of deadly sulfuric acid fill the sky. The air is so thick that the pressure at the surface is a crushing 90 times higher than on Earth.

On Venus, the Sun rises in the west and sets in the east.

Venus

Earth

GREENHOUSE EFFECT

Venus' dense atmosphere traps the Sun's heat, raising the surface temperature to over 864 °F (462 °C). That's hot enough to melt tin and lead.

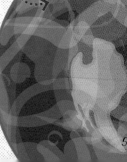

EARTH AND MOON

The Moon is slowly drifting away from Earth, at about the same speed that your fingernails grow.

Earth's day is getting longer as the Moon's gravity gently slows our planet's rotation.

Earth is the densest planet in the solar system.

You are moving through space at around 67,000 mph (107,200 kph)—that's about 100 times faster than a passenger jet.

It takes approximately 27 days for the Moon to orbit (circle) the Earth.

The temperature of Earth's core is around 10,800 °F (6,000 °C)—as hot as the Sun's surface.

Scientists think that the Moon formed when a Mars-sized space rock smashed into Earth around 4.5 billion years ago.

A day on the Moon lasts as long as its year. Because our satellite spins at precisely the same speed as it orbits Earth, we only ever see one side of the Moon.

Amazingly, the Moon is exactly the same size in the sky as the Sun. Our star is about 400 times wider than our Moon, but is around 400 times farther away.

Gravity on the Moon is about a sixth of what it is on Earth. Visit the Moon and you instantly lose five-sixths of your weight!

6

MARS HAS THE SOLAR SYSTEM'S
MOST AMAZING SIGHTS

Pack enough food and a spare spacesuit!
We're off to see the sights on Mars.

HOME OF THE GODS

Olympus Mons is the largest volcano in our solar system. This mountain of rock is 370 miles (600 km) across and towers 14 miles (22 km) high. That's two-and-a-half times as tall as Mount Everest, the highest mountain on Earth. Scientists think the volcano may still be active.

MARTIAN
GRAND CANYON

The 2,500-miles (4,000-km) long Valles Marineris puts the USA's Grand Canyon to shame. This massive rift in the planet's surface is 4 miles (7 km) deep at its lowest point.

TOM HANKS AND MEG RYAN ARE ASTEROIDS

Astronomers have great fun thinking up wacky names for rocks in space.

There are perhaps as many as 1,000 asteroids that could have a finger on us. Yikes!

SPACE ROCKS!

There are millions of rocks spinning through space. These floating fragments, called **asteroids**, are left over from the formation of the solar system. Most of this rocky space rubble orbits the Sun between the orbits of Mars and Jupiter. This band of tumbling stones is called the Main Belt.

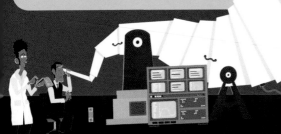

OTHER GREAT ASTEROID NAMES:

9007 James Bond

2309 Mr. Spock

7470 Jabberwock

30269 Anandapadmanaban

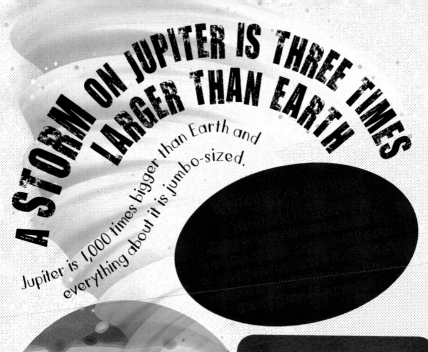

A STORM ON JUPITER IS THREE TIMES LARGER THAN EARTH

Jupiter is 1,000 times bigger than Earth and everything about it is jumbo-sized.

OLD TIMER

With no solid ground to slow them down, storms on Jupiter blow for a very long time. The Great Red Spot was first spotted in 1830 and it has been raging since then, but it may have been blowing for 350 years or more!

JUPITER HAS THE MOST MOONS

Of all the planets in the solar system, Jupiter has the largest number of moons, with a total of 63. The next planet with lots of moons is Uranus, with 27.

The four largest moons of Jupiter are called the **Galilean moons**. These icy worlds were discovered by the famous Italian scientist Galileo in 1610.

1 IO

Io bubbles over with volcanoes, which shoot out fountains of lava and plumes of icy sulfur into space.

2 EUROPA

Mini Europa is covered in sheets of ice. However, scientists think a liquid ocean where life may lurk lies beneath its frozen surface.

3 GANYMEDE

Ganymede, the solar system's largest moon, is bigger than Mercury.

4 CALLISTO

Pockmarked with craters, Callisto is a dead world that looks much like our own Moon.

65

SATURN WOULD
FLOAT IN WATER

Saturn may be the solar system's second-largest planet, but it is made of light gases.

HUGELY LIGHTWEIGHT

You can't stand on Saturn. It is made of hydrogen and helium (the same light gas that goes into party balloons). Those gases are lighter than water, meaning it would float. But who has a tub big enough?

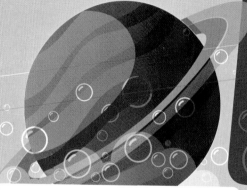

ROCKY RINGS

Saturn's rings are enormous, but very thin, at less than 0.6 miles (1 km) thick. They are not solid, but are made of dust, rocks, and chunks of ice—some as big as houses.

URANUS WAS NEARLY CALLED
PLANET GEORGE

Here's the story of how Uranus got its funny name

Greek God Uranus

1781 Uranus is discovered by English astronomer William Herschel. It has been spotted before, but has always been mistaken for a star. Using a telescope, he realizes it is a planet.

1783 Herschel calls his discovery "Georgium Sidus" after King George III. In 1783, "George" is recognized as a planet.

1850

The other planets in our solar system are named after gods from Greek mythology. Johann Bode changes its name to "Uranus"— after the Greek god of the sky.

Uranus orbits the Sun on its side.

IT RAINS DIAMONDS ON NEPTUNE

Neptune is the king of bling. On this icy giant planet, uncut diamond "hailstones" rain from the sky.

HARD RAIN

Neptune is a frozen world far, far away from the Sun. Its atmosphere contains lots of frozen methane. On Earth this is the natural gas we burn in boilers, heaters, and ovens in the home. But squeezed in the dense atmosphere of Neptune, it turns into solid diamonds, leading to extremely hard rain showers!

BLOWN AWAY

Neptune has the strongest winds in the solar system. Frozen methane clouds whip across the skies at speeds of more than 1,200 mph (2,000 kph).

PLUTO IS SMALLER **THAN THE** USA

When NASA's New Horizons spacecraft flew by Pluto in 2015, it took the first accurate measurements of this dwarf planet.

PINT-SIZED PLUTO

Pluto is 1,473 miles (2,370 km) in diameter. This tiny orb could easily fit onto the mainland of the USA, which is about 2,800 miles (4,500 km) wide.

DOWNGRADED

In 2006, Pluto lost its status as a planet. Because it lacks the bulk to sweep its orbit clean of space rocks and other debris, it was demoted to the status of dwarf planet.

SOLAR SYSTEM STROLL

A hike around Pluto's equator would be 4,627 miles (7,445 km)—roughly the same distance as from Anchorage, Alaska, to Mexico City.

69

SPACECRAFT
MISSIONS

The *Apollo 13* crew set the record for going farthest from Earth: 248,655 miles (400,171 km).

Fruit flies were the first living creatures in space — they went up in 1947.

Astronauts report that space smells like seared steak, hot metal, and welding fumes. Yummy!

The first living thing to orbit Earth was a Russian dog called **Laika** in 1957.

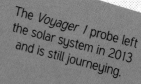

The *Voyager 1* probe left the solar system in 2013 and is still journeying.

Astronauts on the *International Space Station* drink their own (recycled) sweat, breath, and even pee!

Astronauts get taller in space. The spine expands when it's not being pulled down by Earth's gravity.

You couldn't survive in space without a spacesuit for more than 30 seconds.

Valeri Polyakov holds the record for the longest stay in space: 437 days and 18 hours.

Astronauts in orbit around Earth see a fresh sunrise every 90 minutes.

OUR GALAXY HAS A
BLACK HOLE
AT ITS HEART

A black hole is a place in space where gravity is so strong that not even light can escape.

Black holes are not empty. They contain a huge amount of material squeezed into a tiny space. Because light cannot escape their gravity, they are invisible—but they can be detected by their effect on matter nearby.

Black holes come in three sizes:

DARK STARS

Star-sized black holes formed when dying stars collapse. They have ten times the Sun's mass in a space the size of New York City.

TINY TYKES

As big as a single atom, but containing more mass than a mountain.

SUPERSIZE!

Supermassive black holes are giants with the mass of a million Suns. Our galaxy has one at its heart.

OUR GALAXY IS ON A COLLISION COURSE

In 4 billion years the Milky Way will crash into the Andromeda Galaxy.

LIGHT SHOW

Rather than a sudden crash, the galaxies will gently merge. As the distances between stars are so large, hardly any will actually collide. However, future astronomers will be able to enjoy a billion-year-long light show.

GALACTIC CRASH

Our galaxy, the Milky Way, and the the large spiral galaxy Andromeda are currently about 2.5 million light years apart. Drawn by each other's enormous gravity, they are hurtling toward each other at a blistering speed of more than 328,000 ft (100,000 m) per second.

APPROACH SPEED:
249,791 mph
(402,000 kph).

EVERY SECOND SOMEWHERE IN THE UNIVERSE,
A STAR EXPLODES

Massive stars go BOOM! at the end of their lives. These spectacular explosions are called **supernovas**.

GOING SUPERNOVA

In the first 10 seconds of a supernova explosion, a dying star produces more energy than our Sun will release in its 10-billion-year lifetime. For a short time, a single star burns with more energy than a whole galaxy!

A STAR IS BORN

Dying stars go out in a blaze of glory. They burn brightly for weeks, looking like a new star appearing in the night sky. In a galaxy the size of the Milky Way, a supernova happens about every 50 years.

WILL THE SUN EXPLODE?

No. Our star is not massive enough to go supernova.

PULSAR STARS WERE MISTAKEN FOR ALIENS

Pulsars are a type of neutron star—the remnants of a gigantic supernova explosion.

SPACE SIGNALS

Jocelyn Bell discovered the first pulsar in 1967. Scientists thought that the pulsar's flickering signal might be a signal from aliens.

P-P-P-PULSING PULSARS

When a massive star explodes in a supernova, its core collapses inward to form a new, super-dense neutron star. Neutron stars send a beam of radio waves out of each pole. When seen from Earth, this beam blinks on and off like a lighthouse, as the star spins around.

A teaspoonful of neutron stars would weigh 6 billion tons (5.4 billion tonnes).

THE UNIVERSE BEGAN WITH A BIG BANG

Scientists think that everything began with a bang 13.8 billion years ago! All the matter in the Universe exploded out of a tiny dot.

SOME LIKE IT HOT

This surprising idea, that the Universe expanded in a hyper-hot explosion, has three key things going for it:

✓ The amounts of hydrogen and helium in the Universe are as predicted by the Big Bang theory.

✓ All galaxies far away from each other appear to be moving further apart. The Universe is expanding.

✓ Heat left over from a colossal ancient explosion can still be detected in all areas of the sky.

EVERY STAR IS A
TIME MACHINE

The farther away objects are in space, the older they are.

LOOKING INTO THE PAST

Light from stars takes time to travel across space and arrive at our eyes. So, we never see a star as it is "right now." We always see it as it was a long time ago.

BACKDATED SUNLIGHT

It takes light 8 minutes and 19 seconds to travel from the Sun to Earth. If it suddenly shut down, we wouldn't notice until about eight-and-a-third minutes later. The nearest star to the Sun, Proxima Centauri, is 4.25 light-years away. That means it takes 4.25 years for light to travel from Proxima Centauri to Earth.

THE UNIVERSE IS GETTING BIGGER

Finding out that the Universe is expanding is one of the most important discoveries ever.

our expanding Universe

the Big Bang

HUBBLE BUBBLE

In the 1920s, US astronomer Edwin Hubble realized that there was more to our Universe than just our Milky Way galaxy. He found that more galaxies lay outside the Milky Way and they were moving away from us.

GALLOPING GALAXIES

Even stranger, the farther away the galaxies were, the faster they were moving. This means that at one point in time, everything in the Universe was squashed together in one spot.

THERE IS SOMETHING WRONG
WITH OUR PICTURE OF THE UNIVERSE

We can neither see nor understand what makes up most of the Universe.

IN THE DARK

All the galaxies, black holes, stars, planets, moons, and anything else we can see make up just 4 percent of the Universe. These are all made of the stuff we call matter. But there is another mysterious type of matter we know little about—**dark matter**. It acts like normal matter, but it's invisible and (as yet) undetectable.

This is our best guess.

- 4% matter
- 23% dark matter
- 73% dark energy

MYSTERIOUS FORCE

Even more baffling to scientists is **dark energy**. This is a kind of "antigravity" that is pushing the Universe apart.

EARTH IS A GIANT MAGNET

Pull out a compass and watch as the needle swings toward the North Pole. You are picking up Earth's unseen magnetic field.

GIANT GENERATOR

Earth's inner core is mostly solid iron, but it is surrounded by a churning outer core of liquid iron. The molten metal creates electrical currents, and these in turn generate an enormous magnetic field.

FORCEFIELD

Earth's magnetic field extends into space. This invisible forcefield protects us from dangerous charged particles streaming from the Sun.

outer core

inner core

POLES APART

The actual North Pole (Earth's most northerly point) and the **Magnetic North Pole** (where a compass needle points) are not in the same place. The magnetic pole moves about, but they are currently about 310 miles (500 km) apart.

EARTH SPINS FASTER AT THE EQUATOR
THAN IT DOES AT THE POLES

This fact is a head-scratcher. How does the planet avoid unscrewing itself?

DISTANCE DIFFERENCE

Because Earth is ball-shaped, it is widest around its middle. The planet rotates on its axis once every day. To make a full turn, an object on Earth's equator has to travel farther than something near the poles. Since a day lasts the same time on all parts of the planet, the equator must turn faster to keep up.

FEELING DIZZY?

The distance around the planet's equator is roughly 24,855 miles (40,000 km) and Earth completes one full rotation every 24 hours. At the equator, an object spins at a dizzying 1,000 mph (1,664 kph).

AT ITS CORE, EARTH'S ROCKS ARE GOOEY

Earth has a solid crust of hard rocks, but beneath it, things get a little stickier.

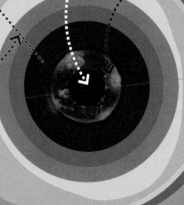

solid

liquid

mantle

crust

INSIDE EARTH

Our planet is layered like an onion. Starting with the gassy atmosphere, each layer gets more dense the deeper you go. The solid crust is made of light rocks. Beneath this is the **mantle**, which is 1,800 miles (2,900 km) thick, making up six-sevenths of Earth's volume.

HOT STUFF

It gets hotter the deeper inside the planet you go. This makes rocks go soft. Mantle rocks are not liquid, but they can move slowly, like putty.

MOST OF EARTH'S GOLD IS TRAPPED IN THE CORE

Gold is extremely rare in Earth's crust, but there is more in the middle.

DISAPPEARING ACT

When Earth formed, the entire planet melted. Heavy elements, such as iron and nickel, sank through the hot, sticky ball of liquid, ending up at the core. Elements such as cobalt, platinum, iridium, osmium, and gold, which love bonding with iron, all but disappeared from Earth's outer layers, too.

BLING COMETS

Scientists think that much of the gold and precious metals in Earth's surface rocks was brought to the planet by comets.

All the gold ever mined would fit into a cube with 67-ft (20-m) sides with a base that would cover two tennis courts and weigh 181,000 tons (165,000 tonnes)

85

VOLCANOES AND EARTHQUAKES

Earth's crust has eight major plates and many smaller plates, which fit together like a jigsaw puzzle.

Plates move about the same speed as your fingernails grow. Most earthquakes are triggered when plates move.

Tsunamis are caused by underwater earthquakes. Ocean swells travel at nearly 600 mph (1,000 kph), and when they hit land, waves over 100 ft (30 m) high cause devastating destruction.

Over three-quarters of Earth's volcanoes are on the rim of the Pacific Ocean, called the "Ring of Fire."

Volcanoes can form quickly. In 1943, Parícutin in Mexico grew into a five-story-high hill in a week. By the end of the year it was 1,102 ft (336 m) tall.

There are around 1,500 active volcanoes today, and nearly 1 in 10 people live within the danger zone of an active volcano.

The longest quake ever recorded was the 2004 Indian Ocean earthquake, which lasted 10 minutes.

In Japanese mythology, a giant catfish called Namazu causes earthquakes when he slaps his mighty tail.

GRANITE IS THE WORLD'S MOST
COMMON ROCK

On land, granite rules. It forms the roots of all the continents.

TAKEN FOR GRANITE!

Granite is resistant to weathering. This hard rock forms some of the most unusual and recognizable landscapes on Earth.

GRANITE ABOUNDS

You can see granite just about everywhere. It's used for sculptures and monuments, on the shiny fronts of banks and offices, on countertops, and in fancy bathrooms.

BIG HEADS

The giant heads of US presidents at Mount Rushmore are carved out of solid granite. Workers removed 441,000 tons (400,000 tonnes) of rock over 14 years—mostly with dynamite. They may last 7 million years.

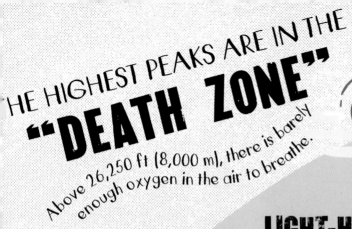

THE HIGHEST PEAKS ARE IN THE "DEATH ZONE"

Above 26,250 ft (8,000 m), there is barely enough oxygen in the air to breathe.

LIGHT-HEADED

The lack of pressure up on the "roof of the world" means that the body does not take in enough oxygen. This causes altitude sickness, which has symptoms that include headaches, nausea, and problems with thinking straight. This can be dangerous, which is why climbers often use oxygen tanks at these heights.

NO EXTRAS

Inside the "death zone," most climbers carry oxygen tanks. However, some climbers still make ascents without oxygen. In 1999, Babu Chiri Sherpa spent 21 hours on the summit of Mount Everest without any extra oxygen.

MOUNT EVEREST IS NOT THE TALLEST MOUNTAIN

Don't trust everything you read! Everest may be the highest mountain above sea level, but it might not be the tallest . . .

MEASURING MOUNTAINS

Mount Everest measures nearly 29,520 ft (9,000 m) from sea level to summit, but it stands on the high Tibetan plateau. Everest itself is 17,060 ft (5,200 m) from its base.

Kilamanjaro, in Tanzania, sits on the African plains and is a longer climb. It is 18,372 ft (5,600 m) from its base to the summit.

When measured from its base on the seabed, Mauna Kea on Hawaii's Big Island is 33,456 ft (10,200 m) tall.

THE WORLD'S DEEPEST GORGE
WOULD FIT 20 EIFFEL TOWERS

20 Eiffel Towers stacked top to bottom would fit
neatly inside Tsangpo Canyon in Tibet.

GRANDER CANYON

At its deepest, Tsangpo Canyon reaches
19,714 ft (6,009 m). That's more than
three times deeper than the USA's Grand
Canyon—or 13.5 Empire State Buildings.

MANY NAMES!

Tsangpo Canyon is also known as
Yarlung Zangbo Grand Canyon
and Brahmaputra Canyon.

"EVEREST OF RIVERS"

The Yarlung Tsangpo River is Tibet's "Everest of
Rivers." Eventually reaching the Bay of Bengal
1,800 miles (3,000 km) away, it first traverses
Tsangpo Canyon. At 314 miles (504.6 km), this
gorge is also longer than the Grand Canyon.

THE ATMOSPHERE AND CLIMATE CHANGE

Two-thirds of Earth's atmosphere is within 5 miles (8 km) of the surface.

An average cloud weighs the same as 80 elephants.

The official boundary of space is 62 miles (100 km) above Earth's surface.

Earth's weather occurs in the thickest layer of the atmosphere, closest to the ground.

Jet streams are speedy air currents that blast around the globe at speeds up to 200 mph (321 kph).

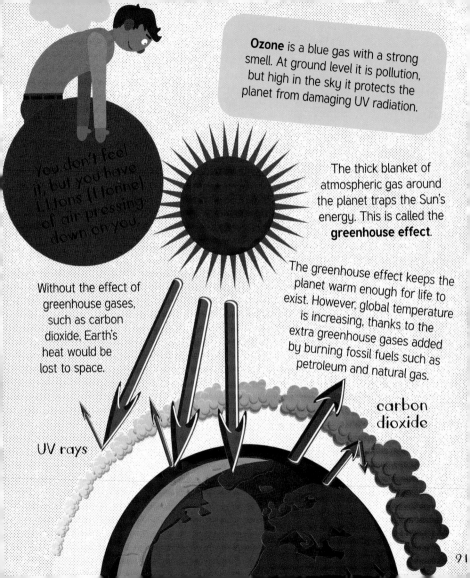

Ozone is a blue gas with a strong smell. At ground level it is pollution, but high in the sky it protects the planet from damaging UV radiation.

You don't feel it, but you have 1.1 tons (1 tonne) of air pressing down on you.

The thick blanket of atmospheric gas around the planet traps the Sun's energy. This is called the **greenhouse effect**.

Without the effect of greenhouse gases, such as carbon dioxide, Earth's heat would be lost to space.

The greenhouse effect keeps the planet warm enough for life to exist. However, global temperature is increasing, thanks to the extra greenhouse gases added by burning fossil fuels such as petroleum and natural gas.

carbon dioxide

UV rays

91

SUNSTORMS MAKE LIGHTS IN THE SKY

Dancing lights above Earth's poles reveal the planet's magnetic secrets.

ALL AGLOW

The northern and southern lights hang like shimmering curtains in the skies close to Earth's poles. Called **auroras**, they are made when fast-moving protons and electrons smash into gas molecules in the upper atmosphere, causing the gases to glow.

SAVE OUR PLANET!

Our star constantly hurls energetic particles into space. This "solar wind" would destroy our atmosphere and wipe out life, were it not for Earth's magnetic field. This invisible forcefield protects the planet by pushing away or trapping most of the particles and cosmic rays.

AT EARTH'S POLES IT IS ALL TIMES

The globe is divided into equal parts from North Pole to South Pole.

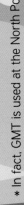

* In fact, GMT is used at the North Pole.

PRIME MOVER

POLE PUZZLER

Walk north and, eventually, you will get to a place where all directions point south—the North Pole. What's the time here? Since this point doesn't move at all, in theory, it is all times here.*

Earth's sunniest place
HAS 4,000 HOURS OF SUNSHINE A YEAR

Yuma, Arizona, is officially the world's sunniest place.

Sunshine city

With over 4,015 hours of sunlight out of a possible 4,500 hours of daylight, Yuma never has less than 8 hours of sunshine a day. That's a 90 percent chance of sunshine . . . every day!

LAND OF THE MIDNIGHT SUN

May on Ellesmere Island is the sunniest month of the year anywhere. This is one of the most northerly settlements on Earth, where in summer the Sun never drops below the horizon. This Canadian outpost averages about 16.5 hours of sunshine per day.

LIGHTNING DOES STRIKE TWICE

Who says lightning never strikes twice? The Willis Tower in Chicago gets struck by lightning up to 100 times a year!

ZAPS FROM ABOVE

Lightning is an electric current from the sky. Static electricity in clouds causes electrical charge to build up on the ground, often on the tallest object. When a connection is made, electricity flashes between the ground and the clouds.

A single bolt of lightning contains enough energy to cook 100,000 pieces of toast.

INCREDIBLY UNLUCKY, OR AMAZINGLY LUCKY?

Roy Sullivan, a US park ranger, was hit by lightning seven times between 1942 and 1977. He survived every single strike.

95

DEATH VALLEY
IS THE WORLD'S HOTTEST PLACE

Walking outside after 10 a.m. is not recommended in these baking badlands.

SCORCHIO!

Death Valley, USA, holds the official record for the highest air temperature. It's 134°F (57°C), measured on July 10, 1913.

CALIFORNIA HEAT

High temperatures are not the only unique thing about the largest national park in the USA outside Alaska. At 282 ft (86 m) below sea level, Badwater Basin is a low point—the USA's lowest in fact!

Putting down roots

Thirsty plants in Death Valley shoot roots 100 ft (30 m) into the ground to slurp up whatever water they can find.

THE CHILLIEST PLACE ON EARTH
IS ANTARCTICA

In 2013, NASA satellites measured temperatures of -135.8 °F (-94.7 °C) here.

BRING AN EXTRA JUMPER

It's no surprise that this frozen continent is the coldest place on Earth. Temperatures in Antarctica are so cold that scientists use a breathing tube that pipes air up their coatsleeves to warm it before they take it into their lungs.

SHIVERING STATION

Until the NASA measurements, the lowest recorded temperature was a bone-chilling -128.6 °F (-89.2 °C). This was measured on the ground at the Vostok Research Station.

MAD DASH

To stave off the boredom, Antarctic researchers dare each other to do naked sprints through the snow in toe-curling -100 °F (-73 °C) temperatures!

97

The world's windiest place
IS ANTARCTICA

ICY BLASTS

In 1913, an Antarctic expedition stopped at Commonwealth Bay. In July, the winds here hit 95 mph (153 kph). It's actually very hard to measure wind speed in the Antarctic, as when it really blows it tends to destroy the equipment!

AUSSIE BREEZE

In 1996, an unmanned weather station on Barrow Island, Western Australia recorded the strongest gust of wind ever, which tipped 253 mph (408 kph).

Oklahoma's "Tornado Alley," in the USA's heartland, is the home of the twister. In April 2011

A HURRICANE RELEASES THE SAME ENERGY AS 10,000 NUCLEAR BOMBS

Born at sea, these swirling summer thunderstorms create havoc when they hit land.

HEAVYWEIGHT DESTRUCTION

Hurricanes pack a powerful punch. The winds alone generate 1.5 terrawatts of power. It also takes lots of energy to evaporate seawater to form clouds and rain. All together, a tropical cyclone has 600 terrawatts of power—that's 200 times the output of all the world's power stations, or as much as 10,000 nuclear bombs!

GENERAL RELEASE

The problem with comparing hurricanes with bombs is, of course, that hurricanes release their energy across a wide area while bombs release it all at once in a very small space.

INDIA HAS THE WORLD'S WETTEST VILLAGE

Meghalaya, in India, is officially the soggiest state in the world.

MONSOON MADNESS

Mawsynram, a village in Meghalaya State, soaks up an average of 467.4 in (11,872 mm) of monsoon rains every year.

BRIDGES

You've got to be smart to live somewhere so wet. Workers wear huge shell-shaped hats made of bamboo and banana leaves. Wooden bridges rot away, so riverbanks are linked by knotting the roots of rubber trees together.

DRIPPY COMPETITION

Only 9.32 miles (15 km) from Mawsynram is Cherrapunji, the second wettest place in the world. This town has an average annual rainfall of 463.7 in (11,777 mm).

THE WORLD'S LARGEST DESERT
HAS NO SAND

Home to penguins, seals, and scientists, Antarctica is a barren wilderness of snow.

POLAR DESERT

Believe it or not, the frozen continent of Antarctica is actually the biggest desert on Earth. Encased in ice, this landmass covers 5.4 million miles^2 (14 million km^2), an area that's 1.5 times the size of the USA.

BONE DRY

Deserts are places that receive less than 10 in (250 mm) of rain in a year. They have very little vegetation. Any plants and animals that live there must survive a harsh, waterless climate.

10

71% OF EARTH'S SURFACE IS COVERED IN WATER

Nearly three-quarters of our planet's surface is flooded.

WATER WORLD

Our planet sloshes with liquid water. Almost all of it (about 96.5%) is salt water in the seas. Water also fills the sky as water vapor and clouds, runs in rivers and lakes, and is stored in ice caps, glaciers, and underground aquifers. Living things are, also, mostly water.

THE WATER CYCLE

Water never stays still. The planet's water constantly moves from the sea to the sky, falling as rain that feeds rivers and fills aquifers. It changes from one form to another.

rain or snow

seawater

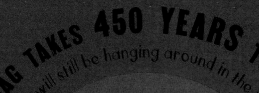

A PLASTIC BAG TAKES 450 YEARS TO BREAK DOWN

Your plastic trash will still be hanging around in the year 2600

A SHOT OF SUNSHINE

Microorganisms can't break down plastic products, but plastic bags and bottles do decompose in sunlight. UV rays break chemical bonds, and the plastic slowly breaks into smaller and smaller pieces.

An estimated 1 trillion plastic bags are thrown away every year.

GIANT GARBAGE PATCH

Plastic discarded into the Pacific is carried on ocean currents to The Great Pacific Garbage Patch, an area as big as Texas. The plastic is broken down into tiny micro-plastic shards and swirls in great, murky clouds, releasing toxins into the water that pose a danger to sea creatures.

A person may contain
100 TRILLION CELLS

Your body contains countless microscopic building blocks, some say up to 100 trillion.

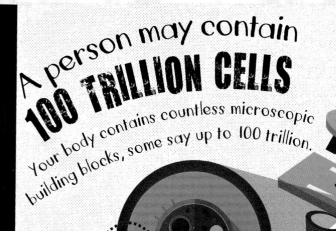

The membrane is like a bag around the cell.

BUILDING BLOCKS

All living things are made of **cells**. You need a microscope to see them. These tiny, self-contained units are surrounded by a membrane that acts like the walls of a house. It keeps unwanted things outside, while inside is a watery liquid that contains all the chemicals needed to make the body work.

HOW BIG IS A TRILLION?

A trillion is a million million, or 1 followed by 12 zeros. If you counted non-stop from one to a trillion, at a rate of one number every second, it would take you about 32,000 years!

1 ... 2 ... 11,024 ... 22,222 ...

YOU ARE MOSTLY
MADE OF BACTERIA

You carry around almost ten times more bacterial cells than your own body cells.

There are more living things on your skin than there are humans living on the planet.

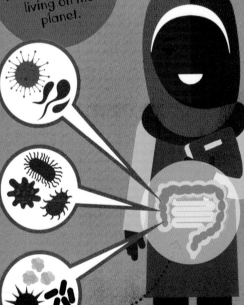

guts

ALIEN LIFE

Most of the cells in your body don't actually belong to you! But don't worry—bacteria actually keep you healthy. In fact, without all these alien germs, you probably wouldn't last long. Most of them live inside your guts and are very useful. They help you break down the food you eat.

GUT FEELING

All these extra microbes weigh as much as 3 lbs (1.4 kg).

There is enough DNA in your body to
STRETCH TO PLUTO AND BACK

And not just once—no fewer than 17 times!

JUST HOW MUCH DNA IS THAT?

There are 3.7 billion miles (6 billion km) between Earth and Pluto. Going at speeds of up to 51,000 mph (83,000 kph), it took NASA's New Horizons spacecraft 10 years to reach Pluto. If it went at that speed along your DNA, it would take 323 years to reach the end.

SPACE SAVER

Every cell of your body contains tightly coiled DNA inside its nucleus. If you unwound the DNA in one cell, it would stretch a staggering 6 ft (2 m). Don't try this at home!

YOU HAVE FEWER GENES THAN A TOMATO

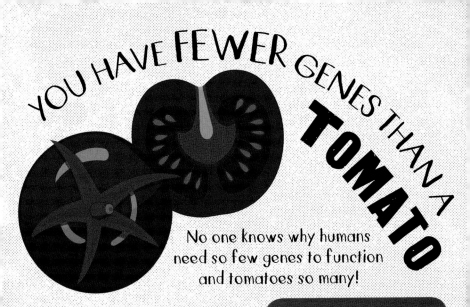

No one knows why humans need so few genes to function and tomatoes so many!

Grape mystery

Genes are strings of DNA that act like the code in a computer program. They are instructions that tell your body how to operate and grow. The number of genes in a living thing varies from species to species. Humans have about 20,000 genes–that's more than a chicken and fewer than a grape, and about the same number as a humble nematode worm!

GENE COUNT

Chicken–16,736 genes
Grape–30,434 genes
Tomato–31,760 genes

HUMANS ARE MOSTLY WATER

Your body is sloshing with liquid.

Soggy cells

You are a giant bag of water! Or more like lots of tiny bags of water, because most of the liquid in your body is found inside cells. Each of the 100 trillion cells in your body is about two-thirds water.

WHERE'S THE REST OF THE WATER?

An average-sized body has about 4 gal (14 l) of water outside its cells. This includes the liquid part of blood, the fluid surrounding the brain and spinal cord, the liquid of the eyes, joint lubricant, and lymph—a watery liquid surrounding cells.

A newborn is about three-quarters water.

YOU ARE STARDUST

The chemical building blocks that make up your body come from exploded stars.

THE UNIVERSE IS IN US

Your body is built from stuff found on this planet, but most of it originally comes from the stars. Matter is made up of simple chemical substances called **elements**. Almost every element was formed in the core of an old star.

NUCLEAR SECRETS

Nuclear fusion reactions in the hearts of stars join atoms of hydrogen together to make heavier elements. When stars run out of hydrogen they sometimes blow up. These spectacular explosions spread new chemical elements across space.

YOUR BODY CONTAINS ENOUGH IRON
TO MAKE A 3-IN (7-CM) NAIL

Most people have about 0.16 oz
(4.5 g) of iron in their bodies.

IRON IN THE BLOOD

About half of the iron in your body is
found in your blood, where it is used
to carry oxygen to your cells. The rest
is dotted around in places such as the
liver, spleen, and bone marrow.

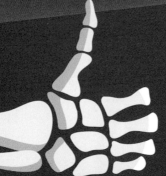

METAL DETECTION

As well as iron, you also
contain about 2.2 lbs (1 kg)
of calcium in your bones
and teeth. That's enough
to make more than 18,000
chalk sticks.

THERE'S ENOUGH CARBON IN YOUR BODY TO MAKE 4 BAGS OF CHARCOAL

Your body and charcoal both contain carbon.

BBQ TIME!

Grab your BBQ tongs and an apron! While oxygen makes up nearly two-thirds of your body weight, it is almost entirely locked up in water. The chemicals of life and the structures of your cells are based on the element carbon. You have about 22 lbs (10 kg) of carbon inside you—that's plenty for a good cook-out.

Vegetarian option

You have enough carbon in your body to make 9,000 pencil leads.

111

IN THE BLOOD

Red blood cells make blood look red.

Adults have about 11 pints (5 l) of blood.

Blood is never blue. Your veins look blue because only blue light penetrates the skin deep enough to be reflected by the veins.

About a quarter of the cells in your body are red blood cells.

Blood carries oxygen and nutrients to your body cells and takes away waste.

A red blood cell makes a complete circuit of your body in just a minute.

Oxygen-carrying blood in arteries is bright red; blood not carrying oxygen in veins appears darker.

The liquid part of your blood, called **plasma**, is actually yellow!

One drop of blood contains about 250 million oxygen-carrying red blood cells.

Your body makes 2 million new blood cells every second.

113

Stretched out flat,
YOUR LUNGS WOULD COVER A TENNIS COURT

Your lungs keep you supplied with oxygen and get rid of waste gases that build up in the body.

A tennis court measures 78 × 36 ft (23 × 11 m).

WHOLE LOTTA LUNG

Your lungs' job is getting gas into and out of your bloodstream. They maximize the contact area between your blood and the air. Inside each lung are 300 million tiny air sacs, called **alveoli**, each covered by a network of small blood vessels.

Your left lung is a little smaller than your right. This is to leave room in the chest cavity for your heart.

BABIES HAVE AROUND 70 MORE BONES THAN ADULTS

Adults have 206 bones in their bodies. Babies have 270. So how come babies' bodies are so wonderfully soft?

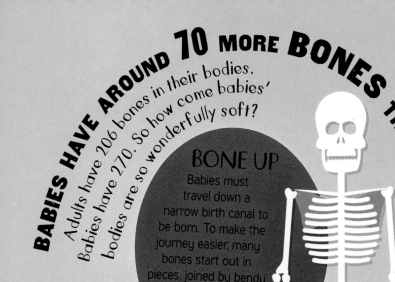

BONE UP

Babies must travel down a narrow birth canal to be born. To make the journey easier, many bones start out in pieces, joined by bendy cartilage. Later, this cartilage hardens into bone.

SQUISHY SKULLS

A newborn baby's skull bones are not yet fused together. Cartilage between the bones allows the skull to squish. That is why many newborns have funny-shaped heads!

THE SMALLEST BONE
IN THE BODY IS PEA-SIZED
Listen up! The smallest bones are inside your ear.

'Ear 'ear

Your ear has an unusual and elaborate mechanism to carry vibrations in the air to your brain. The flappy outer part of your ear channels sounds down your earhole, where the air beats on the thin skin of the eardrum.

eardrum

hammer

anvil

stapes

MINI BEATS

Behind the eardrum, in your middle ear, three tiny bones transmit vibrations to the inner ear. Here, the shaking movements are turned into nerve impulses that get sent to your brain.

The stapes bone looks like a riding stirrup. It measures about 0.12 x 0.1 in (3 x 2.5 mm).

Bones are four times
STRONGER
THAN CONCRETE

Your bones are made of one of the strongest materials known in nature.

STRONG STUFF

Just 1 cubic inch (16 cm³) of bone can take a load of 8.3 tons (7.25 tonnes) without breaking—that's more than the weight of five pickup trucks.

BROKEN BONES

Broken bones have the ability to grow and heal themselves. Arm bones are the most commonly fractured bones in the body.

BABIES CAN BE BORN WITH TEETH

Most babies are just born with gums, but on rare occasions they arrive with a tiny tooth as well.

Smile like no other

Usually, babies don't get their first tooth until they are about six months old. But some lucky parents get a shock when their newborn smiles at them . . . and shows a shiny white tooth! Only about one in every 2,000 babies is born with a tooth.

A GIANT GRIN

The record for the most teeth at birth belongs to Sean Keaney of Newbury, UK. He was born with 12 teeth.

Tooth enamel is the hardest material in the body.

YOU GET TWO
SETS OF TEETH

Your teeth bite and mash food, and are vital for your health.

1. BABY BITES

Babies grow milk teeth between four and seven months of age. By three years old, most kids have a full set of 20 baby teeth.

2. BIG BITERS

When you reach five or six years old, your milk teeth start to fall out, making way for a total of 32 adult teeth. This is your final set of teeth, so take care of them!

3. OLDER AND WISER?

The last four adult teeth grow later than the rest. Wisdom teeth usually arrive between the ages of 17 and 21.

THE HUMAN BODY HAS 650 MUSCLES

Your muscles are the densest, heaviest parts of your body.

heart

PULLING PARTNERSHIP

Skeletal muscles work in pairs to help you move. They are connected to bones with tough tissues called **tendons**. As a muscle contracts (gets smaller), it pulls a tendon connected to a bone. That pulls the bone with it.

Terrifically toned

Your heart is a muscle. In any given day it beats about 100,000 times.

OPEN AND SHUT CASE

The strongest muscles in the body are your **masseters**—the ones that close your jaws.

tongue

FLEXIBLE FRIEND

The tongue is the only muscle in the body that is attached at just one end. A bundle of eight muscles, it moves flexibly like an elephant's trunk.

Some kids can turn their FEET BACKWARD

Are you "double-jointed?"

The medical term for "double-jointed" is hypermobility.

BENDING OVER BACKWARD

It's not unusual to have one or more joints with a greater than normal range of movement. Some people can even dislocate their joints and pop them back in place, allowing them to bend parts of their bodies into crazy shapes. **Hypermobile joints** are caused when the ligaments and tendons, which hold a joint in place, are loose.

FLEXIBLE FEET

Maxwell Day of the UK is a real bendy kid. He can swivel his feet around 157 degrees, which is just 23 degrees shy of pointing directly backward!

MORE FACTS TO DIGEST

Your digestive system breaks down food and drink into parts it can use, and gets rid of the waste.

stomach

intestines

Breaking down food begins in the mouth with chewing and saliva. You make more than 2 pints (1 l) of saliva every day.

Your **digestive tract** is a tube that runs from your mouth to your bottom. It is about 33 ft (10 m) long—almost as long as a school bus.

Your guts are divided into small and large intestines.

The small intestine absorbs most of the nutrients from food. Water is recovered in the large intestine, before the waste leaves your body.

Chemicals made by the liver, pancreas, and gall bladder turn food and drink into nutrients that the body can use as fuel.

Your guts are also packed with bacteria. The gases they release make you fart.

The surface area of your small intestine is about ten times greater than that of your skin.

It normally takes six-to-eight hours for a meal to pass through your body.

In 2009, Michele Forgione produced a record-breaking belch in Reggiolo, Italy. His epic tummy rumble lasted 1 minute, 13 seconds!

TAPEWORMS CAN SURVIVE INSIDE HUMANS FOR 25 YEARS

Hold onto your stomach, this gets gruesome!

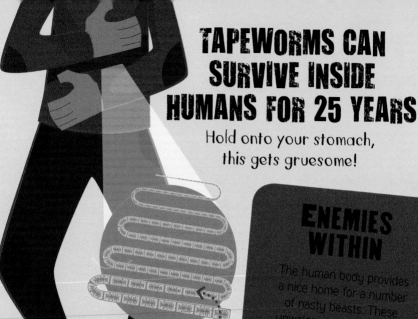

tapeworm

ENEMIES WITHIN

The human body provides a nice home for a number of nasty beasts. These unwelcome tenants range from worms that live in the intestines and feed on the food you eat, to itchy mites that graze on your skin.

FREELOADER

A **parasite** is an organism that lives on or in another living thing, and gets its nourishment from it without any benefit to its host.

SUPERWORM

The world's longest parasite is the tapeworm. In 1991, doctors pulled a tapeworm that was 37 ft (11 m) long out of Sally Mae Wallace's body.

One man had hiccups for 68 years

This is... hic... the... hic... sad story of Charles Osborne. Hic!

PIG OF A DAY

One morning in 1922, American farmer Charles Osborne hiccupped while weighing a hog and began the longest bout of hiccups ever recorded.

HICCUP HELL

At 40 hiccups per minute, Osborne hiccupped around 429 million times!

A WELCOME BREATHER

Osborne's hiccups mysteriously vanished a year before he died.

WHAT IS A HICCUP?

Hiccups happen when your diaphragm—a thin muscle layer under your lungs—suddenly and uncontrollably tightens. This makes you breathe in sharply, snapping shut the opening between your vocal cords and producing a high-pitched "hic."

YOU COULD FILL A TANKER TRUCK
WITH PEE

Urine luck—this is your golden ticket!

GOLDEN GLORY

Depending on how much you drink, you produce about 3.2 pints (1.5 l) of urine a day. That's enough to fill six-and-a-half bathtubs every year.

FILL IT UP!

You may make around 9,500 gallons (36,000 l) of urine in a lifetime. This isn't enough to fill most public baths, let alone an Olympic-sized swimming pool. It is, however, enough to fill a tanker truck.

IN THE PINK

Eating beetroot can turn your pee pink.

A LIFETIME OF FARTS
COULD FILL MORE THAN 2,000 SOCCER BALLS

You let rip about 14 times a day!

A REAL BLOWOUT!

French farty-pants Joseph Pujol could blow out a candle from several paces away with his mighty bottom burps.

Girls and boys pump around 1 pint (500 ml) of stinkers per day. In a year, that's 84 pints (180 l)—enough toots to fill a space hopper!

127

Think your liver is your largest organ? Think again!

SAGGY, BAGGY SKIN

Covering the entire body, **skin** is your largest organ. As well as containing your insides in a nice, flexible package, it protects you from bumps and bruises, and keeps out infectious bugs. Skin also plays a crucial role in keeping you cool.

An adult's **skin** weighs around 8 lbs (3.6 kg).

NEW FOR OLD

Cells in the skin's base layer constantly divide to make new copies of themselves. As old skin cells flake off, they move to the surface. Your skin replaces itself about every month.

layers of the skin

fat

128

SOME PEOPLE CAN HOLD THEIR
BREATH FOR 20 MINUTES

Without special training, people can last 90 seconds before taking a breath.

DIVE! DIVE! DIVE!

Mammals have a dive reflex that is triggered when the face goes underwater. The heartbeat slows and blood is rerouted from the limbs to the head and chest.

Competitive breath holding

Freediver Aleix Segura Vendrell, from Spain, holds the world record for breath-holding. On February 28, 2016, he held his breath for 24 minutes and three seconds. Before the attempt, he breathed pure oxygen.

DEEPEST DIVE

In 2016 Alexei Molchanov dived without air tanks (but with fins) to an incredible 423 ft, 2 in (129 m).

If a man never shaved,
HIS BEARD COULD BE TWICE HIS HEIGHT

Is there a maximum length for whiskers?

WILD WHISKERS

The record for the longest beard on a living person belongs to Sarwan Singh, from Canada, whose facial hair reached a startling 8 ft, 2.5 in (2.495 m).

BIG BEARD

Those Singh whiskers are nothing, however, compared to the beard of Hans N. Langseth (1845–1927). He was known for his 17 ft, 6-in (5.33-m) beard, which he wrapped around a corncob and tucked in a pouch!

LONG CHOPS

The record for the longest beard on a woman belongs to Vivian Wheeler, whose muttonchops measure a striking 10.04 in (25.5 cm).

130

YOU HAVE CREEPY CRAWLIES LIVING ON YOUR FACE

Your eyelashes and eyebrows are home to eight-legged micro-mites.

MIGHTY MITES

Meet **Demodex**. This critter lives on your face. Measuring 0.01 in (0.3 mm) long, it looks like a tiny finger with short, stubby legs at one end. Demodex mites are harmless and bury themselves head-down in hair follicles, peacefully eating the oils we secrete. At night, they come up to crawl around on the surface and meet other mites.

Demodex

NOT ME?

Sorry. Recent studies have shown that 100% of adults have mite DNA on their faces!

YOUR PILLOW IS FULL OF
BACTERIA AND BUGS

What lies underneath your clean and fresh pillowcases?

The stuffing of nightmares

After two years, scientists calculate that a third of the weight of your pillow is made up of germs, dust mites, dust mite poop, and dead skin cells. Sweet dreams!

dust mite

FEELING FLAKEY

Tough old skin cells at the surface of your skin flake off all the time. In just one minute, about 30,000-40,000 skin cells fall off your body. That adds up to about 9 lbs (4 kg) of dead skin cells shed every year—the same as a bag of barbecue coals.

When you blush, YOUR STOMACH BLUSHES TOO

Toe-curling embarrassment is also belly burning.

RUSH OF BLOOD

Blushing is the pink that can spread across your face when you are embarrassed. This reaction is linked to your brain's response to a stressful situation. Although a social mistake isn't dangerous, your body reacts as if it is and releases a chemical called **adrenaline**. Adrenaline makes blood vessels widen, bringing more oxygen to your cells in case you need to run or fight. With more blood rushing through it, your skin turns redder.

BLUSHING BELLY

The prickly heat you feel crawling across your cheeks is also happening inside. Your stomach is surrounded by small blood vessels as well, and so the adrenaline has the same effect.

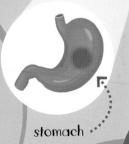

stomach

133

BRILLIANT
BRAIN

The brain accounts for just one-fiftieth of your bodyweight, but it gobbles up a fifth of the energy.

The average brain weighs 3 lbs (1.4 kg) or about as much as 15 candy bars.

Your brain has roughly the same texture as soft tofu.

Although it is just 0.08 in (2 mm) thick, the outer layer of your brain would be as big as a pillowcase if it was spread out.

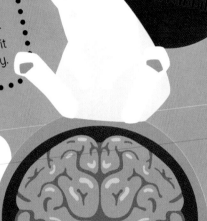

The outer surface of the brain is wrinkled and folded up to squeeze lots of grey matter into the tight space under your skull.

The human brain is over three times as large as the brains of other mammals of equal body size.

Your brain buzzes with electricity, and produces enough to power a 12-watt lightbulb.

The brain has no nerve endings of its own. This means it cannot sense when it is in pain—special pain receptors have to tell it.

Your brain contains about 200 trillion connections. That's about 1,000 times the number of stars in the Milky Way.

You are the only person in the entire world with your exact set of brain connections. This makes you unique.

If you untangled the billions of extremely thin nerve fibers in the brain, they would wrap around the planet four times.

YOU HAVE NEARLY 46 miles (75 km)
OF NERVES IN YOUR BODY

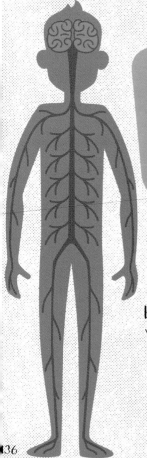

NERVOUS NETWORK

Your nerves constantly carry electrical and chemical signals, zapping messages around your body. They provide your brain with information on the outside world and the state of your insides. They also control your muscles and essential body processes.

SENSITIVE SKIN

The most sensitive bits of your body are where nerve endings cluster together. A thumbnail-sized patch of skin contains around 50 nerve endings.

The brain contains about 100 billion microscopic nerve cells.

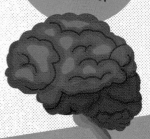

Nerve signals travel faster
THAN A RACING CAR
Your body certainly knows how to deliver a message fast!

SUPER SPEED

Nerves operate at different speeds. Your fastest nerve fibers transmit messages at about 250 mph (400 kph)–faster than the speediest racing car.

Built for speed

Your fastest nerve fibers carry reflexes. They are coated in a fat called **myelin** and can transmit signals 20 times quicker than other nerves. They carry pressure and pain signals so you automatically move away from harm.

UP AND RUNNING

By the time you are four years old, your nerves are at full speed. Newborn and toddler nerves run at about half speed.

ONE WOMAN SNEEZED
FOR 976 DAYS

These jets of air expel problems from the nose.

For about one in five people, bright lights cause uncontrollable sneezing.

WHY DO YOU SNEEZE?

Sneezes get your airways clean. When something gets up your nostrils, your body releases chemicals called **histamines**. This is what starts the tickle in your nose, which won't stop until you produce a mighty honk!

Achoo! Achoo!

Sneezes often come in twos and threes. This happens when a sneeze fails to expel the source of irritation from your nose. Multiple achoos are more common with allergies.

A SINGLE COUGH SHOOTS 3,000
DROPLETS OUT OF YOUR MOUTH
Feel the full force of a cough!

The average cough would fill a 3-pint (1.5 l) bottle with air.

Cover your mouth!

Air shooting out of the lungs produces a jet over 3 ft (1 m) long. It carries thousands of tiny droplets of spit, so it's no surprise that coughing spreads germs.

A TYPICAL COUGH:

✓ Deep in-breath of air.

✓ Air is compressed in the lungs.

✓ An explosive burst, as powerful chest muscles force out air in less than a second.

YOUR TONGUE HAS ABOUT 10,000 TASTE BUDS

Most taste buds are on the tip of the tongue.

TASTE SENSATION

Tiny taste buds, invisible to the human eye, cluster around the small bumps on your tongue. Each bud has around 50 to 150 taste-receptor cells, which send taste nerve signals to your brain.

You can sense just five basic tastes—bitter, sweet, salty, sour, and umami (a meaty flavor).

TONGUE-TASTIC

Californian Nick Stoeberl is the proud owner of the world's longest tongue. His title-winning tongue measures 3.97 in (10.1 cm) from its tip to the middle of the closed top lip.

There are taste buds on the roof of your mouth, in your throat, gullet, and even inside your guts.

THERE ARE MORE BUGS IN YOUR MOUTH THAN PEOPLE ON EARTH

Microbes love your mouth!

HOME SWEET HOME

Your mouth is heavenly for bacteria. There's yummy, sugary food aplenty, no shortage of water and a constant temperature of 97.7 °F (36.5 °C).

A person might have as many as 200-300 different species of microbe in his or her mouth. In all, scientists have identified more than 615 different types of bacteria in people's mouths.

CLEAN THOSE TEETH!

Just one drop of saliva has over 100 million micro-bugs. Depending on the individual— and how often they brush their teeth— there could be anywhere between 100,000 and 1 billion bacteria living on each tooth.

YOUR EYES SEE THINGS UPSIDE DOWN

The lens in your eye flips the image you see.

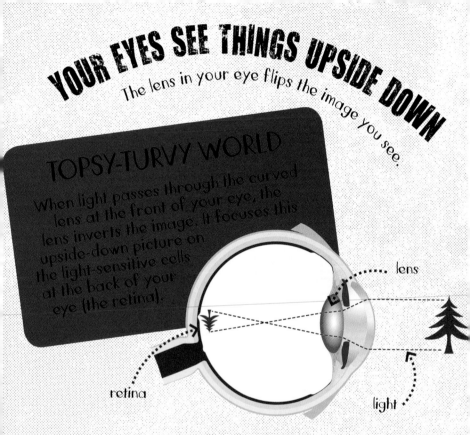

TOPSY-TURVY WORLD

When light passes through the curved lens at the front of your eye, the lens inverts the image. It focuses this upside-down picture on the light-sensitive cells at the back of your eye (the retina).

lens

retina

light

WHY DOESN'T THE WORLD LOOK UPSIDE DOWN?

Your brain is smart enough to fix the upside-down image. Psychologist George Stratton proved this in the 1890s. He wore a set of reversing glasses that flipped his vision. For the first four days, he saw the world upside down, but on day five the world turned the right way up again.

EVERY HUMAN HAS A BLIND SPOT

The middle of your view is missing.

FIND YOUR BLIND SPOT

1 Fold a piece of paper in half.

2 Draw a small "X" on the right side, 2.5 in (6 cm) from the fold.

3 Draw a small dot on the left side, 2.5 in (6 cm) from the fold.

4 Hold the paper in front of you and close your right eye . . .

5 Keep your eye on the dot and slowly move the paper away from you. The "X" magically disappears!

HOLE IN ONE

Light-sensitive cells line the eye's back wall. They send information to the brain via the optic nerve. But there are no light sensors where the optic nerve connects to the eye. Your brain has to fill in what's there by looking at the surrounding area.

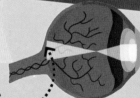

blind spot

143

YOUR EARS AUTOMATICALLY CLEAN THEMSELVES

You shouldn't need to clean them any other way.

GOLDEN GLOOP

Your ears produce a yellow wax. This sticky and shiny stuff stops the skin of your ear canal from drying out, fights off infections, and protects your eardrums. This gloop traps things that get into your ear, mopping up dust and dirt.

CHEERS EARS!

You don't need to get rid of earwax. Every motion of your jaw moves old earwax toward the opening of the earhole. Eventually, wax falls out naturally or is washed away.

The world's hairiest ears belong to Radhakant Bajpai of India. His tufts measure 5.2 in (13.2 cm).

YOUR EARS HELP YOU KEEP YOUR BALANCE

Ears do more than just hear!

LOOPY LABYRINTH

Deep within your inner ear, a strange, snail-like organ, called the **cochlea**, helps you to keep your balance. The cochlea's spirals are filled with fluid, and above it are three small loops, called semicircular canals. These are also filled with liquid and tell your brain the position of your head. Movement in the fluid in the loops signals to your brain that you are moving.

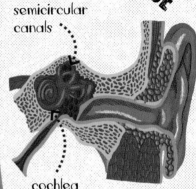

semicircular canals

cochlea

EAR BE GIANTS

The world's strongest ears are Manjit Singh's. He pulled a 7.5-ton (6.8-tonne) passenger plane a distance of 13 ft (4 m) with his ears.

LEFT-HANDERS ARE MORE
SUCCESSFUL AT SPORTS

The key is that most people are right-handed.

SOUTHPAW SUCCESS

Handedness, preferring to use one hand over the other—is a uniquely human trait. Nearly 90 percent of people in the world are right-handed. Just 10 percent of people are left-handed. This means that in sports lefties have lots of practice playing right-handed opponents, but the "righties" encounter left-handed opponents much less often. This gives left-handers an advantage, and perhaps explains the high sporting triumphs.

NOTHING SINISTER...

We get the word "sinister" from the Latin word for left.

FAST RUNNERS HAVE LONGER TOES THAN MOST PEOPLE

Long toes help athletes push off with lots of force.

TOE TIME

When they reach top speed, elite sprinters' feet hit the ground for as little as 0.1 seconds, so pace is about moving with as much power as possible in that brief time.

In the 100-m final of the 2008 Olympics, Jamaican Usain Bolt ran with a shoelace untied ...and he still set a new world record!

GIANT STRIDES

Usain Bolt is the fastest person on the planet. At full speed he takes a gigantic 8 ft (2.5 m) step. Over 328 ft (100 m) he takes just 41 steps.

149

TIME TO ACT YOUR AGE

Four babies are born every second somewhere in the world.

When your mother was born, she was carrying the egg cell that would become you.

An average baby triples in weight by his or her first birthday.

If you kept growing at the rate of your first year, by the age of 20 you'd be a 24.5-ft (7.5-m) giant who weighed 309 lbs (140 kg)!

By the time you are six years old, your brain is nearly fully grown.

Babies can't shed tears until they are about 8 months old.

Both boys and girls get hairier during puberty.

Babies' brains have more connections than adult brains.

As you become an adult, your skin produces more oil, so you get more pimples.

The wearing down of protective cartilage pads in leg joints and between spine bones can knock 2 in (5 cm) off your height by the age of 70.

ONE IN EVERY FIVE CHILDREN SLEEPWALKS

No one really knows what causes sleepwalking.

NIGHT WALKS

Sleepwalking is sitting up or wandering around while fast asleep. People don't actually walk with outstretched arms, like a zombie! However, they often look vacant, as if no one is at home.

TO WAKE OR NOT TO WAKE?

Sleepwalkers can put themselves in danger, but many people won't wake them. Don't worry— waking a sleepwalker won't give him or her a heart attack. Perhaps the best thing to do, is to lead a sleepwalker gently back to bed. They won't remember a thing in the morning!

You have 2,000 DREAMS A YEAR

These mysterious experiences may be nothing more than your brain cells firing randomly while you catch some "z"s.

We spend one-third of our lives asleep. In an average lifetime, this adds up to about 25 years of napping.

DREAMTIME

You might have five or six dreams in a single night. You will have forgotten them by the time you wake up. No one really knows what causes dreams, or why they happen.

SLEEPYLAND

New surroundings cause us to wake more often, making us more likely to remember dreams. This gives us the impression that we dream more when we travel.

CHEMICALS
CONTROL HOW WE FEEL

FEELING EMOTIONAL

When you feel happy or sad, angry or weepy, you are experiencing **emotions**. They are short bursts of mental activity that help you react to situations. Anger or fear set your heart racing, send blood to your most important organs and get you ready to fight or flee. Messenger molecules called **hormones** flood into your blood to organize your body's response to these complex feelings.

disgust   happiness   fear

sadness   anger   surprise

There are six basic emotions that are common to humans. People everywhere can recognize a look of anger, disgust, fear, happiness, sadness, or surprise on someone's face.

NO ONE KNOWS WHY WE LAUGH

You most often laugh when something catches you off-guard, but scientists don't know exactly why this is!

Kids laugh about three times more than adults.

TICKLED PINK!

Humans aren't the only animals that laugh. Chimps enjoy a chuckle and rats give a high-pitch squeak of delight when tickled!

YOU'RE HAVING A LAUGH!

Tickling, funny jokes, or talking to friends does something very strange to humans. It can cause spontaneous spasms of the diaphragm, which make us gasp, giggle, or guffaw!

EVERYTHING IS MADE OF ATOMS

Atoms are the basic building blocks of everything around you.

MATTER MATTERS

An **atom** is a tiny particle of matter. Invisible to all but the most powerful electron microscopes, these tiny units are always jiggling and moving about. They join together in unimaginably vast numbers to build all the big stuff of our world.

ATOMIC IDEAS

Ancient Greek philosopher Democritus came up with the idea of atoms. However, they weren't discovered until the 20th century.

There are something like 7 million billion trillion atoms in the human body.

ATOMS ARE MOSTLY
EMPTY SPACE

99.9% of an atom's mass is in the nucleus.

MINI SOLAR SYSTEM

Atoms are made of three different kinds of minuscule particles—positively charged protons, neutral neutrons, and negatively charged electrons. The protons and the neutrons stick together extremely tightly in the atom's core. Powerfully attracted to this positive nucleus, the electrons orbit around it. Even though this picture isn't 100% accurate, it's a useful way to imagine an atom.

The number of protons decides what type of atom, or "element" it is.

The number of protons and electrons is usually balanced, so that an atom has no overall charge.

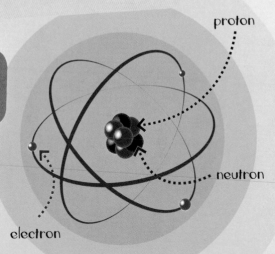

proton

neutron

electron

ELECTRONS ARE RESPONSIBLE FOR ALL CHEMISTRY

New substances are made when atoms combine.

FREE AND EASY

Protons and neutrons are buried in the atom's nucleus. Tightly bound together, they can only be separated by powerful energy, such as nuclear reactions. Electrons are more loosely tied to the atom. They hop from one atom to another, get knocked off, or go wandering free. Atoms bond with each other by exchanging and sharing electrons. Joined-together atoms are called **molecules**.

nuclear power plant

CHEMISTRY FUNNY CORNER

ATOM 1
Are you sure you've lost an electron?

ATOM 2
Yes, I'm positive!

200 billion atoms in your body may have
BELONGED TO SHAKESPEARE.

William Shakespeare

TO BE, OR NOT TO BE?

Atoms don't die, but people do. Nature recycles every single atom in your body. And there are plenty to go around, when you count both the atoms in someone's body and the atoms that enter and (ahem) exit during life. Owning a bunch of Shakespeare's atoms doesn't mean you get his genius, though!

Cleopatra

ATOMIC HISTORY

It's not just Shakespeare's atoms. You have billions more from Evita, Elvis, Emily Pankhurst, Einstein, Cleopatra, and Caligula.

Albert Einstein

CHEMICAL ELEMENTS

There are 118 types of atom, called "elements."

The Sun burns up 683 million tons (620 million tonnes) of hydrogen every second.

Astatine is the rarest element found in nature—just 1 oz (30 g) of it exists in the Earth's crust at any time.

Together, the elements hydrogen and helium make up 98 percent of the matter in the universe.

The heavy metals osmium and iridium are twice as heavy as lead!

The most reactive elements are **fluorine** and **francium**.

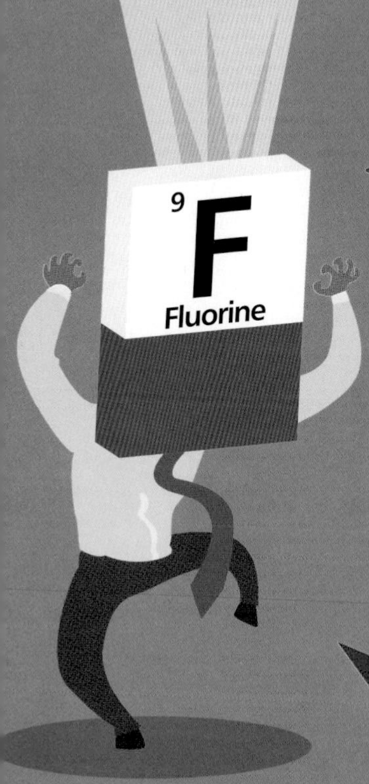

At \$27 million per gram, **californium** is the most expensive element.

⁹⁸ **Cf** Californium

⁹ **F** Fluorine

The element **mercury** is the only metal that is liquid at room temperature.

Just 92 elements occur naturally on Earth.

Hydrogen atoms were made during the Big Bang—this makes them an awesome 13.8 billion years old!

161

J is the only letter that has never APPEARED ON THE PERIODIC TABLE

The periodic table is much more than a list of chemical elements.

HAPPY FAMILIES

Russian superscientist Dmitri Mendeleev devised the periodic table in 1869. It was a way to organize all the known chemical elements into groups that share similar properties. Chemists use the table to predict the kinds of reaction an element will undergo and the sorts of compounds it may form.

Dmitri Mendeleev

SYMBOLIC

Each chemical element has a symbol. H stands for hydrogen, the first element in the table.

Since element 114 ("ununquandium") was renamed **flerovium** (Fl) in 2012, there is no longer a Q in the periodic table.

ONLY ONE PERSON COULD WRITE
HIS ADDRESS IN CHEMICAL ELEMENTS

American chemist Glenn T. Seaborg is still the only person to have had a chemical element named after him while living.

Seaborgium, Lawrencium Livermorium, Berkelium, Californium, Americium.

ELEMENT HUNTER

Glenn Seaborg is top of the element charts with a hand in discovering 10 elements. When he worked at the Lawrence Livermore Laboratories at the University of California, Berkeley, you could send him a postcard addressed using only elements.

SOME METALS EXPLODE ON CONTACT WITH WATER

The group I elements of the periodic table are the most reactive metals.

The group I metals are stored under oil to stop them from reacting with water in the air.

potassium

EXTREME METALS

Drop a small lump of **lithium** into water and the light metal fizzes and jigs on the surface. You hear a hissing sound as hydrogen gas bubbles off. A little pop and the hydrogen gas ignites, while the metal burns with a red flame. The reaction with **potassium** is more energetic—it goes "BANG!" with a beautiful lilac flame! The most violent reaction is with **cesium**.

MORE THAN THREE-QUARTERS OF
OF ALL ELEMENTS ARE METALS

A quirk of matter is that most of it is metallic.

METAL MATTERS

Metals are mostly shiny materials, which reflect light. They are generally amazing at conducting heat and electricity. This is because of the way atoms join together in metals. The outer electrons of each atom are free to drift through the material. This also makes metals very tough, but flexible.

Copper and **gold** are strange because, unlike other metals, they are not silvery.

gold

electric cable

Earth's core contains enough iron to make a train rail that would loop the globe 50 billion times.

All the gold ever mined would fit
INTO A SURPRISINGLY SMALL CUBE*

Gold is a very rare metal in Earth's crust.

Earth's crust

KING OF BLING

Bright and lustrous, gold is the must-have metal that people go crazy for. Because it is virtually indestructible, all the gold that has been dug out of the ground is still with us—although most of it is locked in bank vaults.

YOU CANNOT BE SERIOUS!

The biggest amount of gold found in one place is 550,000 gold bars, stored deep beneath the subway in the vault of the Federal Reserve Bank of New York. It's worth over $200 billion.

*A cube with sides of
67 ft (20 m)

THE FIRST ELEMENT WAS DISCOVERED BY BOILING PEE

It's the 1660s.

Meet Hennig Brand. He was a German alchemist who dedicated his life to finding the **philosopher's stone**. This mythical substance would supposedly turn cheap metals into gold. Hennig reasoned that a golden shade was probably quite important....

... so he chose human pee. No, we're not sure why either. He boiled 50 vats of urine until he got a thick syrup. Hennig Brand's stinky experiments resulted in **phosphorus**—a new element that burst into flame on contact with air. However, it wasn't the philosopher's stone.

Now you'll never forget that phosphorus begins with a "P!"

165

CARBON IS THE MOST VERSATILE ELEMENT

There's something special about the fourth most common element.

USEFUL STUFF

Carbon is great at combining with other elements (and with itself, too). It forms a vast number of substances. Plastics and petroleum products are all carbon compounds! Carbon is added to steel to make it hard, and to resin to make super-light, super-strong, carbon-fiber composites.

ESSENTIAL ELEMENT

All life we know about, from tiny microbes to giant whales, uses carbon-based chemistry. Our bodies rely on molecules built around chains of carbon.

There are more than 10 million known carbon compounds.

An average pencil **CAN DRAW A LINE 38 MILES LONG**

Pencil leads have nothing to do with lead. They are made from a form of carbon called **graphite**.

graphite ·····

DIFFERENT STROKES

All atoms of the same element have exactly the same number of protons. But that doesn't mean they always link together in the same way. Carbon forms crystal-clear and super-hard diamonds—the hardest substance found in nature—deep under Earth's surface. It also forms dark, soft, and slippery graphite. This greasy form of carbon is the one used in pencils.

16

NUCLEAR WASTE STAYS DEADLY
FOR A QUARTER OF A MILLION YEARS

Waste produced by nuclear power stations requires special storage.

STING IN THE TAIL

Nuclear power stations use long rods of radioactive uranium-238 as fuel. Using powerful nuclear reactions, they produce "clean" electricity. Unlike fossil-fuel-burning power stations, they produce no carbon dioxide. There is one major problem, though. Their spent fuel is highly radioactive.

STORAGE PROBLEMS

A large reactor produces 22-33 tons (20-30 tonnes) of waste per year. It's dangerously radioactive. High-level waste is kept in storage pools for 20 years. Then it is packed into strong barrels and buried under the ground.

BANANAS ARE RADIOACTIVE

Bananas contain lots of potassium. Some potassium is radioactive . . .

FEELING FUNNY

Doctors calculate that you would need to eat 10,000,000 bananas in one sitting to die of radiation poisoning, or 274 bananas a day for seven years to notice any effect. Eating bananas isn't going to turn you into a mutant supervillain in a hurry.

TOTALLY BANANAS

Not all potassium atoms are radioactive, just those with 19 protons and 21 neutrons—called K-40. Luckily, only a tiny 0.012% of potassium is dangerous K-40. Each banana contains a miniscule 0.000001 oz (0.0000393 g) of K-40.

169

SUPERCOOLED HELIUM FLOWS UPHILL

Lighter-than-air helium laughs at gravity.

ESCAPE ARTIST

Helium is the fun gas that goes into party balloons. If you breathe it in, it makes your voice go funny and high-pitched. Chill helium to within a few degrees of absolute zero, however, and it does weird things. It runs through the walls of its container and climbs walls. It becomes a superfluid, with cool superpowers!

Helium is the second most plentiful element in the Universe, but it is rare on Earth. It is so light that most of it has escaped into space.

MOST MATTER IN THE UNIVERSE IS PLASMA

We think of Earth as normal. It really isn't.

FANTASTIC PLASMA

Conditions on our planet are so mild that matter is normally in one of three states—solid, liquid, or gas. **Plasma** is known as the fourth state of matter. Plasma only exists where the energy is high enough to tear atoms apart, separating the electrons from the nucleus. On Earth, we only find this in lightning bolts, plasma lamps, and nuclear fusion reactors.

GAS
Free flowing, completely fills any container

steam

LIQUID
Will flow to take the shape of its container

water

ice

PLASMA
The Sun is a ball of plasma.

SOLID
Fills space with a 3-D fixed shape

HOT WATER FREEZES QUICKER THAN COLD WATER

The **Mpemba** effect is a weird phenomenon scientists struggle to explain.

WHAT'S COOLER THAN COOL?

In 1963, Erasto Mpemba discovered that hot ice cream freezes faster than cold ice cream. It made no sense. More tests with his physics teacher confirmed this stranger-than-strange finding. But no one could explain why.

FREEZE TEASE

The ways things freeze is complicated, so the Mpemba effect doesn't always work. Some scientists think it may be caused by the way water molecules push each other away as they cool and get closer together. However, others still argue that the effect is not real.

172

Water expands
WHEN IT FREEZES

This effect is DEFINITELY real, and explains why ice floats in water.

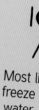

ICEBERG ALERT

Most liquids shrink when they freeze and turn into a solid. Not water. Ice crystals have a more open arrangement of molecules compared to liquid water. As they grow in freezing water, they push outward, expanding the volume by nearly ten percent.

Icebergs that are smaller than 16 ft (5 m) across are known as "bergy bits" and "growlers."

The world's largest iceberg measured 183 miles (295 km) long and 23 miles (37 km) wide, and was larger than the island of Jamaica.

AWESOME OXYGEN

One in five parts of Earth's atmosphere is made up of oxygen.

Oxygen powers the chemical reactions that keep life going on Earth.

Ozone is made of three atoms of oxygen joined together—O_3.

The gas we breathe is made of two atoms of oxygen joined together—O_2.

Oxygen is the most common element on our planet's surface.

High up in the atmosphere a layer of ozone gas protects us from the Sun's damaging UV, or ultraviolet, radiation.

After hydrogen and helium, **oxygen** is the third most common element in the Universe.

Oxygen is so reactive that on Earth it is always found combined with other elements.

Breathing pure oxygen for more than 16 hours is fatal.

Oxygen gas is transparent; liquid oxygen is blue.

Around 300 million years ago, there was so much oxygen in the air that wildfires would have burned even wet plants.

THE WORLD'S STRONGEST ACID IS A
MILLION TIMES STRONGER THAN SULFURIC ACID
Steer clear of superbad superacids!

STRONG STUFF

Superacids are a new breed of chemicals that are trillions of times more powerful than traditional acids. They are used in the chemical industry, especially with crude oil products. **Fluoroantimonic** (say flu-roh-ant-ee-mon-ik) **acid** is considered the strongest of these powerfully reactive substances.

ALIEN ACID

Superacids are not the most corrosive acids. **Hydrofluoric** (say hy-droh-flor-ik) **acid** is like something from a sci-fi film. It eats through almost everything. It even burns straight through glass. Its special plastic containers need changing every two years.

STOMACH ACID IS STRONG ENOUGH TO
DISSOLVE A RAZOR BLADE

However, no one should try this out!

empty stomach

full stomach

digestive system

BAG OF ACID

When you are ready to eat, your belly fills with **hydrochloric acid**—a strong, highly corrosive acid. The acid attacks the chewed-up food that you swallow, but it also attacks your stomach. To prevent damage, the stomach lining produces an anti-acid bicarbonate solution, just like the tablets used to calm indigestion. Even so, the lining needs renewing about every four days.

MULTIUSE MATERIAL

Hydrochloric acid is used in steelmaking, leather tanning, salt production, and in many of the cleaning products you use at home.

steelmaking

177

IF YOU POUR A HANDFUL OF SALT INTO WATER, THE WATER LEVEL GOES DOWN

A real scientific head-scratcher. Try it yourself.

1 Put water in the glass and mark the water level.

4 Check the water level.

2 Carefully add several spoons of salt to the glass.

3 Slowly stir the water until all the salt has disappeared.

WHAT'S GOING ON?

The explanation has to do with the fact that water molecules repel, or push, each other away. Adding salt interrupts this effect and allows the molecules to get closer together, reducing the overall volume of water.

BOTH "HOT ICE" AND "COLD BOILING WATER" ARE POSSIBLE

STRANGE BREW

British climbers complain they can't make a decent cup of tea in high mountains. This is because at lower pressures, water boils at lower temperatures. And tea made in less-than-boiling water does not make a tasty drink. In space, where there is no air pressure, water boils instantly (and then the water vapor freezes instantly).

UNDER PRESSURE

The "Z-machine" in New Mexico can create super-high pressures, about 120,000 times above normal air pressure. Water squeezed so tightly forms ice that is hotter than the boiling point of water.

On the summit of Mount Everest, water boils at 161°F (72°C).

CHEMICAL REACTIONS MAKE NEW SUBSTANCES

Most things around us are not made of single elements. Chemistry is all about how different atoms and molecules interact with each other.

ALL KINDS OF REACTIONS

A chemical reaction happens when one substance changes into another. Sometimes this is irreversible—when you bake a cake, there's no way to reverse the reaction to get back to the raw ingredients. Other reactions can go both ways, from starting materials to products, and back again.

THE NAME'S BOND... CHEMICAL BOND

Atoms join together to make molecules, either by sharing electrons or by taking electrons from each other.

Catalysts boost chemical reactions
MILLIONS OF TIMES

yogurt

TINY HELPER

Catalysts speed up chemical reactions by reducing the amount of energy they need to get going. They help to produce everything from plastics to fertilizers, washing powder, yogurt, cheese, and beer. Protein catalysts called **enzymes** in our bodies allow us to digest food and grow.

cheese

washing powder

fertilizer

Ozone hole

Not all catalysts are welcome. Banned chlorofluorocarbon (CFC) chemicals, which were once used in spray cans, catalyze the breakup of ozone in the upper atmosphere.

CATALYST CLUB

There are strict rules to become a catalyst.

1. Speed up a reaction.

2. Do not get involved in the reaction.

181

CATALYTIC CONVERTERS USE PRECIOUS METALS

These devices, attached to the exhaust pipes of cars, convert toxic exhaust fumes into cleaner gases.

CLEANER CARS

Gasoline and diesel engines produce all kinds of muck, including carbon monoxide, pollution-causing nitrogen oxides, unburned fuel, and soot. The metal catalysts inside a catalytic converter quickly speed up the breakdown of these toxic gases.

OUT
carbon dioxide
nitrogen gas
water vapor

IN
carbon monoxide
nitrogen oxides
unburned fuel

Nitrogen oxides converted to oxygen and nitrogen gas

Catalytic converters contain platinum, palladium, and rhodium—all three are more expensive than gold.

FERTILIZERS QUADRUPLED EARTH'S POPULATION

Artificial fertilizers replace the nitrogen that crops remove from the soil, so the same land can be used year after year.

HABER NITROGEN FIX

Until the invention of artificial fertilizers, farmers piled compost and animal dung on their fields. But nothing was better than giving the soil a break. The Haber-Bosch process changed all that. Invented in the 1900s, it was an industrial method for making nitrogen-rich ammonia. With fertilizers boosting food production, the world's population boomed from 1.6 billion in 1900 to nearly 7.6 billion people today.

We use 221 million tons (200.5 million tonnes) of fertilizer every year.

COOL CHEMISTRY
ACCIDENTAL DISCOVERIES

In the 1830s, Charles Goodyear discovered how to toughen rubber when a mix of rubber, sulfur, and lead dripped onto a hot stove.

The world's most common plastic, **polyethylene**, was invented twice, both times by accident.

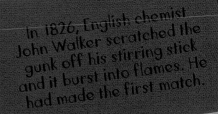

In 1826, English chemist John Walker scratched the gunk off his stirring stick and it burst into flames. He had made the first match.

Spencer Silver tried to make strong glue in 1968, but only got a weak re-stickable adhesive—perfect for sticky little paper messages!

Harry Coover's attempts at making clear plastic gun sights ended up in a powerfully sticky gloop we now call **superglue**.

Stretchy nylon fiber was invented by accident in 1935, when a lab assistant clumsily poured two mixtures together.

Tiny molecular "soccer balls" of carbon atoms, called "buckyballs," were a total suprise to the scientists who discovered them in 1985.

When Roy Plunkett found a heat-resistant, non-reactive slippery powder in an old tube in 1938, he used it to make non-stick Teflon coatings for pots and pans.

Chemist Constantin Fahlberg discovered the first artificial sweetener, saccharin, in 1878, after forgetting to wash his hands before lunch.

THE FIRST ARTIFICIAL DYE WAS DISCOVERED BY MISTAKE

Dyes for cloth used to be made from minerals, plants, or animals.

START WEARING PURPLE

Purple dye was once so rare and expensive to produce, it was the color of Roman emperors and royalty. That was, until the summer holidays of 1856. In his bedroom lab, the teenage William Perkins was looking for a cure for malaria. All he produced was a disappointing black lump. However, when he washed it away, it ran a deep, vivid purple. Perkins had invented **mauveine**, the artificial dye that made him rich.

Before mauveine, it took 12,000 snails to produce enough purple dye for a toga's hem!

The world's most dangerous scientist
WAS THOMAS MIDGELEY, JR.

This well-meaning scientist invented the most dangerous chemicals in history.

LEADED FUEL

In the 1920s, Midgeley pioneered adding lead to gasoline. This made car engines run more smoothly and improved their mileage. Unfortunately, the lead-laced fumes were toxic and damaging to brains. Leaded gas was finally banned in the 1990s.

CHLOROFLUOROCARBONS

Next, Midgeley threatened the planet with **chlorofluorocarbons** (CFCs). Although safer than other chemicals used in refrigerators at the time, these gases destroy ozone high in the atmosphere. In 1985, scientists discovered a huge hole in the ozone layer that protects Earth from the Sun's UV rays.

187

The greatest chemical lifesaver
GROWS ON MOLDY BREAD

Penicillin may well have saved your life. Without it, sore throats and infected cuts can sometimes turn fatal.

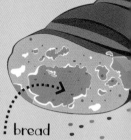

bread mold

DON'T DO THE DISHES

Scottish chemist Alexander Fleming discovered the wonder drug penicillin by accident in 1928. He went on vacation without cleaning his petri dishes. When he returned, he noticed that the mold now growing on these dishes had stopped bacteria in its tracks!

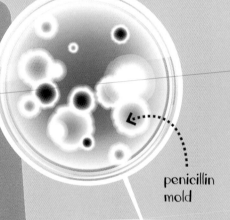

penicillin mold

petri dish

Although he discovered penicillin, Fleming never actually found a good way to extract it. Pals Howard Florey and Ernest Chain finally figured out a way to purify penicillin in 1939.

LIFE IS "LEFT-HANDED"

This is one of the greatest mysteries of life.

MIRROR MOLECULES

Your two hands are the same basic shape, but they are mirror images of each other. Some molecules are like this, too. "Right-handed" molecules look like reflections of "left-handed" molecules.

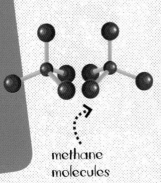

methane molecules

These foods are packed with "left-handed" amino acid molecules.

LEFTIES RULE

Amino acids are the basic building blocks of proteins, the long molecules that are absolutely essential for life. Amino acids can be left- or right-handed, but the ones found in living things are always left-handed. Nobody knows why this is.

ANTISEPTIC WAS FIRST USED BY A SURGEON

All hail Joseph Lister, rescuer of the human race!

HEALTH RISK

Before chemical antiseptics, surgery was very risky. Cuts could easily become infected by bacteria. These invisible microbes caused "ward fever." Even a patient who had a successful operation could later die from the infection.

CLEANING UP

Lister covered wounds with dressings soaked in carbolic acid. He also introduced handwashing, sterilizing instruments, and disinfecting with carbolic spray while operating. The rate of infection plummeted.

BAD OLD DAYS

Before the 1860s, surgeons wore filthy aprons and didn't sterilize their surgical instruments. They didn't always wash their hands before operating, either.

THE FIRST BATTERY WAS INVENTED
2,000 YEARS AGO

Did an ancient civilization invent electrical power?

FIRST BATTERY?

About 200 BCE, in what is now Iraq, a smart inventor built a very special clay pot. Inside was an iron bar, around which was a copper cylinder. This apparatus was bathed in acid and closed with a tar stopper. What this Mesopotamian "battery" was used for is still a mystery.

iron bar

acid

copper cylinder

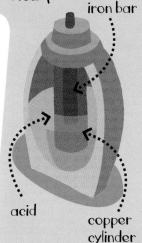

Voltaic pile

copper and zinc disks separated by paper

TOWER OF POWER

Italian scientist Alessandro Volta invented the first modern battery in 1800. This high-tech sandwich of metal disks soaked in saltwater was the first reliable source of electrical energy.

191

MICROCHIP SILICON HAS
"NINE NINES" PURITY

The silicon in computer chips has to be ultra-pure to work.

MAKING THE GRADE

Only the purest silicon—electronic grade silicon—can be used to make silicon chips. The start of the process is making one enormous crystal of silicon, taller than an adult and weighing hundreds of kilos (or pounds). This is then purified, at temperatures hotter than molten lava (2,700 °F/1,500 °C).

"Nine nines" purity = 99.9999999% pure!

WAFER THIN

Microchips are engraved into silicon wafers. Each wafer is cut to 0.04 in (0.5 mm) thick—about the width of a pencil lead, and then polished flatter-than-flat.

The longest chemical name takes
OVER THREE HOURS TO SAY

The chemical name of the longest known protein is also the longest word in the English language.

TITAN TITIN

Titin is not a particularly long word. However, it IS a long molecule. Also known as connectin, the chemical name of this giant protein found in muscles stre-e-e-etches to 189,819 letters long. If you have a spare three and a half hours, you could work out how to say it.

SAY IT AGAIN ...

Supercalifragilisticexpialidocious is a made-up word, but is only 34 letters long. You'd need to say it 5,583 times over to match the length of titin's gigantic name.

193

HARD FACTS ABOUT CONCRETE

Concrete is made of sand and gravel, held together with lime cement.

Concrete gets stronger as it gets older.

There are around 150 billion grains in 1 lb (450 g) of concrete.

When mixed with water, a chemical reaction occurs. Crystals grow, setting the concrete hard.

M·AGRIPPA·L·F·COS·TERTIVM·FECIT

The Romans invented modern concrete.

The Pantheon in Rome is the world's largest unreinforced concrete dome.

The oldest known concrete is about 2,500 years old.

CONCRETE
50 KG
50 KG · 50 KG

The largest continuous concrete pour was enough to fill eight Olympic-sized swimming pools and took four days in 2017, in Sharjah, UAE.

Every 1.1 tons (1 tonne) of cement made produces 1.1 tons (1 tonne) of carbon dioxide.

sticky rice

The Chinese added sticky rice to their concrete mixes when building the Great Wall of China.

China's Three Gorges Dam is the world's largest concrete structure. It was built with 565 million ft³ (16 million m³) of concrete!

195

THIOACETONE IS THE WORLD'S SMELLIEST CHEMICAL

Meet the substance so stinky it makes people pass out.

RUN AWAY!

In 1889, in Freiberg, Germany, a factory attempted to produce **thioacetone**. It caused mass panic! People were fainting and being sick all over the place. They tried to flee town to escape its foul smell.

Just one drop of thioacetone is enough to create a whiff nearly 1,660 ft (500 m) away!

REAL STINKERS

Two other contenders in the stench stakes are:
- Skatole—the smell of poop.
- **Mercaptan**, which is added to natural gas to alert people to gas leaks. It smells of rotting cabbages and smelly socks.

GRAPHENE IS THE WORLD'S
THINNEST MATERIAL

A million times thinner than a human hair, graphene is the world's first 2-D material.

flexible graphene screen

WONDER STUFF

Discovered in 2004, **graphene** is an ultralight, super-flexible material made of a net of carbon atoms arranged in hexagons, just like a honeycomb. In sheets a mere one-atom thick, graphene is transparent, and is the world's best conductor of electricity.

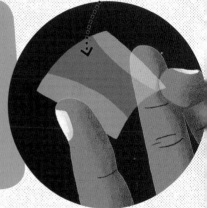

LUCKY ACCIDENT

Graphene was discovered by researchers cleaning graphite samples with tape. Checking the tape, the scientists realized that, along with the dust and dirt, they were ripping off super-thin graphene sheets.

graphene sheet

Graphene is 200 times stronger than steel.

MOST PIECES OF PAPER CAN'T BE FOLDED IN HALF MORE THAN SEVEN TIMES

Try it at home if you dare.

FOLDING BY NUMBERS

An A4 sheet is 12 in (300 mm) long and 0.002 in (0.05 mm) thick.

Each time you fold it, you double the paper's thickness.

By the third fold the sheet is nearly eight times thicker.

At the 30th fold the paper would be 62 miles (100 km) high and in space.

42 folds would get you to the Moon.

At 103 folds, your sheet would be thicker than the observable Universe: 93 billion light-years across!

folding fun!

Britney Gallivan holds the paper-folding world record with 12 folds in a sheet of toilet paper.

CARBYNE IS THE WORLD'S STRONGEST MATERIAL

Another carbon wonder material, carbyne is EVEN stronger than graphene.

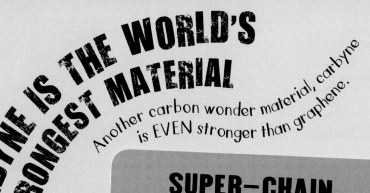

SUPER-CHAIN

Carbyne is made of long chains of carbon just one-atom wide and invisible to the naked eye. Although predicted over 50 years ago, researchers have only recently learned how to make the molecule. In 2014, they joined together a record 6,400 carbon atoms.

OUT OF THIS WORLD

Although it's tricky to make carbyne on Earth, it has been spotted in space. These carbon chains exist on asteroids and in clouds of interstellar dust.

THE WORLD'S STICKIEST GLUE COMES FROM BARNACLES

Barnacle glue sticks to any surface, under any conditions.

STUCK ON YOU

These rock-loving crustaceans are famously difficult to remove, especially when they take up residence on the hulls of boats. **Barnacles** only come to rest when they become adults. Their free-swimming larvae choose a spot on a rock and then release their two-part bio-glue. The bit that goes down first is oily and drives water off the rock surface. The second part sticks them on—tight!

The U.S. Navy reckons that barnacles add as much as two-thirds extra weight to their boats.

AEROGELS ARE THE WORLD'S LIGHTEST SUBSTANCES

This class of materials is mostly made of air.

LIGHT AS AIR

These lightweight substances, nicknamed "solid smoke," start out life as a gel. They are then dried in a pressure vessel, which leaves the solid part intact, but riddled with microscopic holes where the liquid was. **Aerogels** are completely dry to touch.

99.98% of the volume of aerogels is air.

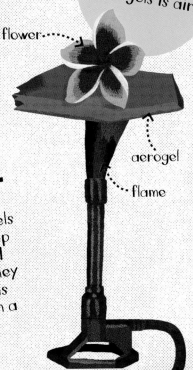

flower

aerogel

flame

SUPER SPONGE

Because they have such a large surface area, aerogels are amazing at mopping up spills. They are also good insulators, meaning that they can protect something as delicate as a flower from a naked flame.

A TRILLION PLASTIC BAGS ARE
MADE EVERY YEAR

REDUCE, REUSE, RECYCLE

16.1 million tons (14.6 million tonnes) of plastic waste goes into the ocean every year.

People love plastic. It's cheap, it's strong, it's super-flexible and can be made into about any shape you require. It can be any color you like, too! Unfortunately, most plastics take hundreds of years to break down. This means plastic waste is building up.

seagull feeding its chick plastic

MICROPLASTIC, MAXI-PROBLEM

In the oceans, plastic bags snarl up turtle flippers. Animals mistake them for food and gobble them up. Sunlight breaks the plastic into tiny particles, which ocean currents swirl into enormous floating garbage patches.

TIGER STRIPES ARE CONTROLLED BY CHEMISTRY

Nature has lots of familiar patterns, but how are they made?

STRIPED SKINS

A tiger's stripes are like fingerprints. No two tigers have exactly the same pattern. Scientists suggest that there might be two types of proteins in a tiger's skin— one that encourages cells to organize themselves a certain way, to make a stripe, for example, and one that blocks this from happening. The interaction between these two chemicals is what forms patterns, from tiger and zebrafish stripes to leopard spots.

Tigers have striped skin, not just striped fur.

leopard

tiger

zebrafish

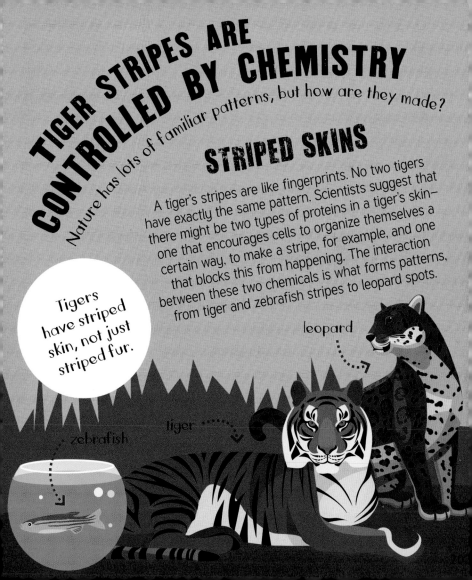

YOU SPEND A DECADE OF YOUR LIFE WATCHING TV.

It's fun to watch TV, but it can be a huge waste of time!

SCREEN TIME

If, like the average person, you spend three-and-a-half hours a day watching TV, that amounts to more than four days every month spent gazing at the screen. A month and a half of TV time every year. Just remember there's something called "outside," and that occasionally you may want to go out and see the world for yourself!

The average American watches about five hours of TV a day.

Indonesia leads the world in screen time.

THERE ARE ABOUT 44,000 RADIO STATIONS WORLDWIDE

Radio waves are a form of electromagnetic energy that crosses vast distances.

satellite

RADIO GAGA

Radio waves are great for communication. TV and radio shows from around the world travel as radio waves. Telephone chat and Internet traffic bounce around the planet via satellites. Radio signals even help us to communicate with space probes on distant planets.

How low can you go?

Submarines use very low frequency (VLF) and extremely low frequency (ELF) radio waves, which can travel through water, to communicate with the surface.

WONDERFUL WIRELESS

Wi-Fi, Bluetooth, and wireless transmissions use extremely high frequency (EHF) radio waves.

205

THE WORLD'S FASTEST CAR CAN
BREAK THE SOUND BARRIER

The Bloodhound SSC looks
like a sharpened pencil with
a rocket strapped to it.

SONIC SPEED

Sound travels through the air at a
speed of 767 mph (1,235 kph). When
something travels faster than the
speed of sound, it creates a loud
sonic boom, like a crack of thunder.

OFFICIAL LAND SPEED RECORD

In 1997, Andy Green
piloted Thrust SSC to a
speed of 763.035 mph
(1,227.985 kph). It also
became the first car to
break the sound barrier.

TOP SPEED

Bloodhound SSC takes just 3.6 seconds to travel 1 mile (1.6 km).
Andy Green hopes to get it up to 1,000 mph (1,609 km/h).

THE WORLD'S FASTEST TRAIN
FLOATS ON SUPER MAGNETS

Faster than a bullet train, maglev trains currently are top of the tracks.

Japan's L0 Series experimental maglev is the world's fastest train with a record speed of 375 mph (603 kph).

MAGLEV

Standing for 'magnetic levitation', maglev trains use superconducting magnets to make the entire train hover 4 in (10 cm) above the track. Gliding on a bed of air, this near-friction-free motion means the train can move like greased lightning.

SUPERCONDUCTORS

These aren't superhero fare-collectors. **Superconductors** are materials that conduct electrical currents with zero resistance. Chilled below -448.6 °F (-267 °C), the temperature of liquid helium, they make incredibly powerful electromagnets.

track

THE LARGEST SHIP IN THE WORLD IS AS LONG AS THE EMPIRE STATE BUILDING IS TALL

These colossal cargo carriers are truly massive.

GIANT TANKER

The supertanker *Knock Nevis* was the largest ship ever built. The 1,500-ft (458-m) monster was scrapped in 2010.

MIGHTY MATZ

The Matz Maersk Triple-E is too big to fit through the Panama Canal. Fully loaded, it carries 18,000 containers. Its propellers weigh a scarcely credible 70 tons (64 tonnes) apiece.

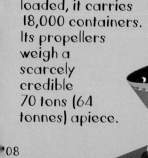

THE LARGEST LAND VEHICLE IS
TALLER THAN THE STATUE OF LIBERTY

Bagger 288 is a monster of a mining machine. Standing 311 ft (95 m), its bucket wheel is as tall as a seven-story building!

GERMAN DIGGER

Working in open-pit mines, this giant excavator chomps dirt with its rotating wheel of buckets. Each bucket holds an almighty 1,717 gallons (6,500 l) of soil. When it hits a seam, it can shift 264,500 tons (240,000 tonnes) of coal per day!

MOVING HOME

In 2001, Bagger had to move to a mine 14 miles (23 km) away. It took three weeks to make the journey.

209

DRIVERLESS CARS CAN DRIVE
IN COMPLETE DARKNESS

Autonomous cars let you kick back, while the car drives itself.

EASY RIDER

In a driverless car, an onboard computer handles the tricky tasks of keeping the car on the road, changing lanes, and passing other vehicles. It tracks lane markings and road edges to keep its wheels pointed in the right direction.

SPLIT-SECOND DECISIONS

It takes 3-7 seconds for a driver to take control, even with warning lights and sounds. A driverless car responds in a fraction of a second.

DRIVING BLINDFOLDED

You are three times more likely to die in a car crash at night than during the day. To improve safety, Ford has pioneered a laser-guided car that drives in the dark.

GPS antennae

camera

LiDAR (light detection and ranging unit)

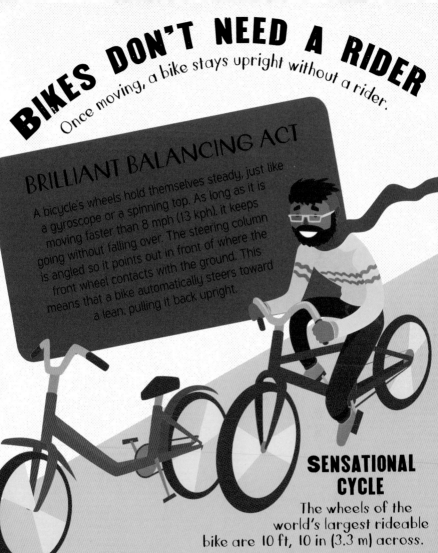

BIKES DON'T NEED A RIDER

Once moving, a bike stays upright without a rider.

BRILLIANT BALANCING ACT

A bicycle's wheels hold themselves steady, just like a gyroscope or a spinning top. As long as it is moving faster than 8 mph (13 kph), it keeps going without falling over. The steering column is angled so it points out in front of where the front wheel contacts with the ground. This means that a bike automatically steers toward a lean, pulling it back upright.

SENSATIONAL CYCLE

The wheels of the world's largest rideable bike are 10 ft, 10 in (3.3 m) across.

SOLAR-POWERED PLANES CAN STAY IN THE AIR FOR MONTHS

A new breed of aircraft runs on sunshine.

CHINESE DRAGON

The Chinese solar-powered drone, **CH-T4**, is huge, but doesn't need a pilot. Designed as a giant flying wing, it cruises 12 miles (20 km) above the ground. Its 131-ft (40-m) wings are as long as three long-distance buses, but the CH-T4 weighs just 880 lbs (400 kg).

This lightweight drone is powered by sunshine, so it doesn't need to refuel.

AROUND THE WORLD

In 2016, **Solar Impulse 2** became the first solar-powered plane to complete a full circuit of the planet.

THE WORLD'S LARGEST AIRCRAFT CAN LIFT A SPACE SHUTTLE

The Antonov An-225 Mriya is the longest and heaviest plane ever built.

RUSSIAN MONSTER MOVER

The wings of this Soviet-era cargo aircraft are nearly as long as a football field. Fully loaded, it weighs the same as six blue whales. Six enormous turbofan engines pull this behemoth into the air. Only one of these giant planes was ever built, in the 1980s. It could carry the Buran space shuttle piggyback. It is still in service today.

The An-225's call sign is "Cossack."

HEAVY LANDINGS

Jumbo jets have 18 wheels. The An-225's landing gear has 32 wheels!

ARCHITECTURAL TECHNOLOGY

Architecture was one of the five arts-oriented events (e.g., music, painting) at the Olympic Games until 1948. Medals were first awarded at the 1912 Summer Olympics in Stockholm, Sweden.

When complete in 2020, the Jeddah Tower in Saudi Arabia will be the first building to reach 0.6 miles (1 km) high.

The Shanghai Tower is world's third tallest building. Its four floors plunge 1/4 ft (86 m) feet underground.

Sidu River Bridge in China has the longest drop from the bridge deck to the ground, with a height of 1,627 ft (496 m).

The 31.3-mile (50.45-km) long Channel Tunnel between France and England has the longest undersea stretch of 23.5 miles (37.9 km).

The Great Mosque of Djenné in Mali is the world's largest mud-brick structure.

Beijing's "Bird's Nest" stadium is the world's largest steel structure, with 22 miles (36 km) of unwrapped steel weighing 121,254 tons (110,000 tonnes).

About 1,000 elephants helped build the **Taj Mahal**, the world's most elaborate tomb.

The Roman aqueduct, **Pont du Gard**, was made without mortar—its some 6-ton (5.4-tonne) stone blocks fit perfectly together.

Looking like a flower from above and a ship from ground level, the Guggenheim Museum in Bilbao is clad with 33,000 extremely thin titanium sheets.

THE WORLD'S TALLEST BUILDING
IS THE BURJ KHALIFA

Three times taller than the Eiffel Tower and nearly twice as tall as the Empire State Building, the Burj Khalifa holds six world records.

Nearly a kilometer high, at 2,716.5 ft (828 m) tall, the **Burj Khalifa** in Dubai, United Arab Emirates (UAE), is the tallest freestanding structure in the world.

The concrete used to build the tower weighs the same as 100,000 elephants.

No fewer than five of the largest passenger planes could fit inside the running up length of the skyscraper.

The Burj Khalifa has the world's longest elevator, ascending 140 floors.

PALM JUMEIRAH
is the world's largest artificial island

Artificial islands are dry land clawed back from the sea.

DREAMLAND

The **Palm Jumeirah** is a weird and wonderful engineering marvel. It is an artificial island in the sea off Dubai, UAE. It covers an area greater than 800 football fields. But even more surprisingly, it is made in the shape of a giant palm tree and surrounded by a circular sea wall.

PLEASANT PALMS

The palm tree is important to the history and culture of the Middle East. It is seen as a sign of hospitality—a warm welcome to guests.

VELCRO® was invented to
MIMIC NATURAL BURRS

This all-purpose fastener is used for clothes, backpacks, and even spacesuits.

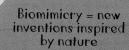

Biomimicry = new inventions inspired by nature

ZIPPERLESS ZIPPER

The hook-and-loop fastener was based on the burr of the burdock plant. These sticky hooks snag onto anything that passes. Swiss engineer Georges de Mestral got the idea in 1941, when his dog came back from a walk covered in burrs. Today, VELCRO® is made from heat-treated nylon. The hooks are made from cut loops.

A small strip of VELCRO® is taped inside a space helmet for use as a nose-scratcher by astronauts.

218

THE FIRST WORDS SPOKEN ON A TELEPHONE WERE, "MR. WATSON, COME HERE."

The story of the phone began on March 10, 1876.

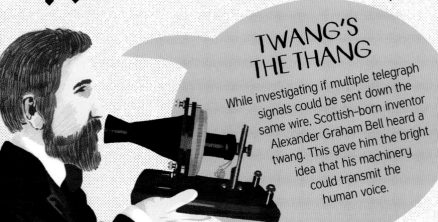

TWANG'S THE THANG

While investigating if multiple telegraph signals could be sent down the same wire, Scottish-born inventor Alexander Graham Bell heard a twang. This gave him the bright idea that his machinery could transmit the human voice.

We can only imagine what Bell would have made of a modern phone!

Ironically, Alexander Graham Bell's mother and wife were both hard of hearing.

MODERN PRESSES CAN PRINT MORE THAN
20 MAGAZINES EVERY SECOND

The first mechanically printed book, the Bible, was made in 1455.

printing press

PRINTING TIME

Pounding through 28 copies per second, with its cylinder revolving 833 times per minute, the fastest printing press in the world knocks out 100,000 copies in an hour. The speediest desktop printers only manage a measly 68 sheets per minute.

The novel, Harry Potter and the Deathly Hallows, holds the record for the largest first printing ever, with an initial run of 12 million copies.

World's smallest book

Measuring just 0.3 in (0.75 cm) across, this Japanese book about flowers through the seasons requires a magnifying glass to read.

THOMAS EDISON TRIED 6,000 DIFFERENT MATERIALS

TO FIND THE PERFECT LIGHT BULB FILAMENT

LIGHTING UP THE WORLD

The first practical bulb was made by US inventor Thomas Edison. He saw that to make a filament glow white-hot it needed to be very thin and poor at carrying electrical current. Edison tried out lots of metals and even beard hair, before settling on carbonized bamboo fiber.

LONG LIFE

The Livermore Centennial Light Bulb in a Californian fire station has burned continuously for over 100 years!

Thomas Edison

Shine bright

Incandescent bulbs are very inefficient. They convert just 2.5 percent of electrical energy into light. Compact fluorescent bulbs are four times more efficient.

A WORLD OF ENERGY

In just one hour, Earth receives more energy from the Sun than we use in a whole year.

Nearly half of the world's electrical energy is produced by burning fossil fuels such as coal and oil.

People in the developed world use far more energy than people in the developing world.

The **carbon footprint** of an activity, process, or product is the amount of carbon dioxide it releases.

Fossil fuels are preserved sunshine—when these once-living things burn, they release the energy that they captured from the Sun while alive.

A single search on Google releases around 0.007 oz (0.2 g) of carbon dioxide.

The biggest blackout in history happened in India in 2012. The outage left 620 million people without power.

The largest hydroelectric plant on the planet is China's **Three Gorges Dam**.

The nuclear fuel uranium is about 8,000 times more powerful per unit weight than oil or coal.

Its 34 turbines generate the same energy as burning 49.6 million tons (45 million tonnes) of coal.

THE WORLD'S BIGGEST TUNNEL-BORING MACHINE
CUTS A HOLE AS WIDE AS A TENNIS COURT

There's nothing boring about these monster machines.

According to tradition, a tunnel-boring machine can't start digging until it is given a name.

BIG BERTHA

Meet Bertha, the world's largest underground hole-cutter. Her cutterheads are as tall as a five-story building. Spinning about once a minute, Bertha's drills bore through solid rock and dirt. In 2013, while digging a 2-mile (3.2-km) tunnel under the streets of Seattle, Washington, she got stuck. It took two years to rescue her.

BIG TO DIG!

Bertha is as long as 29 double-decker buses and weighs as much as 480 regular buses.

224

THE NIF'S MEGA-LASER IS MADE
BY COMBINING 192 LASERS

Artificial star

The National Ignition Facility (NIF) in Livermore, California, uses the world's largest laser to mimic conditions inside stars. When a small pellet-sized target is blasted by its beam, it hits 90 million °F (50 million °C)—nearly six times hotter than the Sun's core. The laser creates a compressing force 150 billion times that of Earth's atmosphere. This flash of energy makes atoms join together, releasing more energy than it took to generate the laser beam.

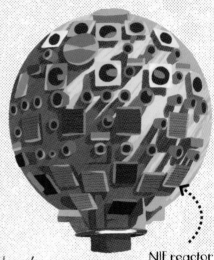

NIF reactor

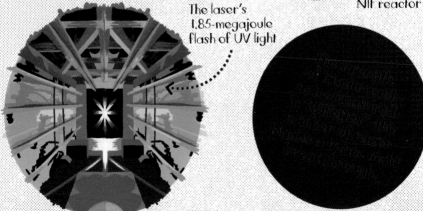

The laser's 1.85-megajoule flash of UV light

STEM CELLS COULD HELP BLIND PEOPLE TO SEE

SUPERCELLS

The human body is made up of some 200 different types of cell. Each of these cell types does a different job. Most cells make exact copies of themselves, but some special cells, called **stem cells**, can morph into almost any type of cell. Doctors harvest these jack-of-all-trade cells and use them to mend damage in the body.

Stem cells help you regrow your entire skin every month.

cone

rod

MIRACLE VISION

Researchers use stem cells to grow sheets of light-sensitive rod and cone cells. In future medical treatments, these could be implanted into eye retinas to help blind people to see.

226

ARTIFICIAL HANDS
CAN NOW BE PRINTED

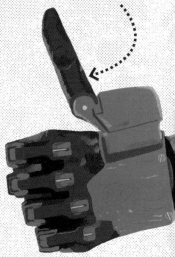

LENDING A HAND

With a digital file downloaded from the Internet, people who have lost a hand, or were born without one, can print out a fully working robotic hand. The 3D-printed plastic hands come in cool, loud shades and look like robot parts. Kids love them and they can get new ones as they grow, because the hands are much cheaper than traditional prosthetics.

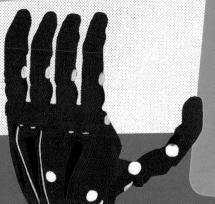

PRINT-A-PART

3D printing builds shapes from the ground up, by laying down layer after layer of melted plastic, squirted out of a tiny nozzle. Slice by horizontal slice, a solid object is built up.

227

THE FASTEST BALL SPORT IN THE WORLD IS JAI ALAI

Three-quarters the size of a baseball and harder than a golf ball, the **pelota** is the speediest ball used in sport.

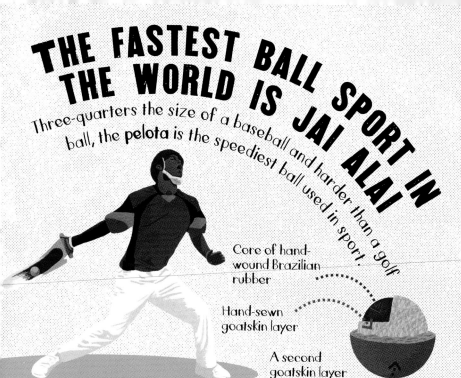

Core of hand-wound Brazilian rubber

Hand-sewn goatskin layer

A second goatskin layer to cover

Jai alai means "a jolly feast" in Basque.

PLAYING CATCH, WITH A CATCH

Playing jai alai takes awesome hand-eye coordination. Players must catch and throw a ball called a pelota with a wicker scoop. Streaking past at 188 mph (302 kph), the pelota is the fastest-moving ball in sport.

HI-TECH TRAINING TOPS CAN NOW
MONITOR YOUR HEART RATE

Wearable tech is the latest buzz.

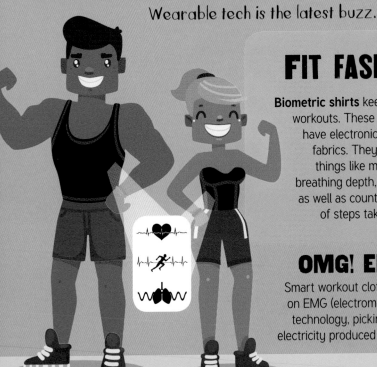

FIT FASHION

Biometric shirts keep track of your workouts. These "smart" clothes have electronics built into the fabrics. They can monitor things like muscle effort, breathing depth, and heart rate, as well as count the number of steps taken.

OMG! EMG

Smart workout clothing relies on EMG (electromyography) technology, picking up the electricity produced by muscles.

CHARGED UP!

Forget running out of juice, a new wave of wearables will charge batteries in your devices by storing the energy of your movement or body heat.

229

THE FIRST MOBILE PHONES WEIGHED AS MUCH **AS A BAG OF SUGAR**

The bulky battery "brick" took 10 hours to charge and only had half an hour of talk time.

BIG BILL

The first cell phones cost around $3,000!

BRAGGING RIGHTS

The first mobile-phone call was made on April 3, 1973.

SNAPS CHAT

Philippe Kahn shared the first picture taken on a phone in 1997. It was a snap of his newborn baby.

FINNISH FAVE

The Nokia 1100 is the top-selling electronic gadget in history, with more than 250 million devices sold.

The average smartphone user touches their phone more than 2,600 times a day.

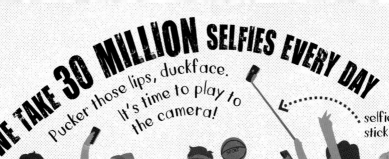

WE TAKE 30 MILLION SELFIES EVERY DAY

Pucker those lips, duckface. It's time to play to the camera!

selfie stick

HERE'S LOOKING AT ME

The selfie is the king of pics. 24 billion of these self-portraits were uploaded to Google's servers in 2015. Be sensible, though. In the same year, more people died taking selfies than were killed by sharks.

The extendable selfie stick was first invented in the 1980s, but it didn't catch on then.

SHOOTING STAR

American astronaut Buzz Aldrin snapped the first selfie taken in space, on his first spacewalk in 1966.

SUPER SLOW-MO CAMERAS
CAN CATCH LIGHT MOVING

Slow-mo photography is endlessly fascinating. It's fun watching water balloons burst, an egg being hit with a hammer, or a dog's ears flapping as it shakes off water in super-slow motion.

OVERCRANKING

It's all about frames per second. **Slow-motion cameras** capture images at a much higher frame rate than normal. When played back at normal speed, the action takes longer to happen. So you can see things your eyes are not usually fast enough to catch.

SUPER-SPEED PHOTOGRAPHY

A "femto-photography" camera is an ultra-fast camera that takes photos one trillion times a second. It can watch a burst of light passing through material and can even see around corners!

THERE ARE NOW MORE THAN 2,500 ARTIFICIAL SATELLITES ORBITING EARTH

satellite

Satellites transmit telephone and Internet communications, carry TV and radio signals, monitor our planet, and spy on us.

Sputnik 1

THE FIRST SATELLITE

The first artificial satellite was Sputnik 1, launched by the U.S.S.R. in 1957. It was about the size of a beach ball and took just over 98 minutes to orbit Earth on its elliptical path. It stayed in orbit for three months before falling into the atmosphere and burning up.

SPACE JUNK

It's not just space hardware up there. The U.S. Space Surveillance Network tracks more than 13,000 items larger than 4 in (10 cm).

The Global Positioning System (GPS) uses a fleet of 24 satellites orbiting 11,500 miles (24,000 km) above Earth's surface.

233

INSIDE THE INTERNET

The Internet is a vast network of computers around the world, all connected together.

Sharks like to chew underwater Internet cables.

The World Wide Web is the information on the Internet —a collection of web pages.

English computer scientist Sir Tim Berners-Lee invented the World Wide Web in 1989.

The Internet connects 3.2 billion people, who access it on 8.7 billion devices.

Data sent over the Internet is broken into small packets. It travels to you via the least congested route and when it arrives, your computer puts it all back together.

The longest submarine cable in the world stretches 24,000 miles (38,600 km) and connects 33 countries.

The gazillions of moving electrons that make up the data-in-motion on the Internet weigh about the same as one strawberry.

SPAM

DELETE

About two-thirds of all e-mails are spam.

Your online data can be anywhere—individual files can be spread across data centers around the globe.

The world's first webcam was trained on a coffee pot at the Computer Laboratory at the University of Cambridge, helping people to avoid a wasted trip if the coffee pot was empty.

THE WORLD'S MOST POWERFUL SUPERCOMPUTER
CAN RACE THROUGH 93 QUADRILLION CALCULATIONS A SECOND

With its 41,000 chips, the Sunway TaihuLight is the world's fastest computer.

Computer speeds are measured in **FLOPS**, which stands for "floating-point operations per second."

PUZZLE–CRACKING PROBLEM–SOLVERS

China leads the world in supercomputers. These titanic machine-brains fill entire warehouses and tackle the biggest problems. They can even calculate the birth and early expansion of the Universe. Supercomputers also try to predict how earthquake waves will travel to find out about the inside of our planet.

calculation per second = 1 FLOPS

2017 iMac = 1,900,000,000,000 flops (1.9 teraflops)

Sunway TaihuLight = 93,000,000,000,000,000 flops (93 petaflops)

COMPUTERS ON BOARD THE APOLLO SPACECRAFT WERE ONLY AS POWERFUL AS TODAY'S CALCULATORS

An average cell phone has vastly more power than the computers that took humans to the Moon and back safely.

A FLYING TOASTER

The computer on board the Apollo spacecraft was more basic than today's toasters. It had just 36 KB of permanent memory—less than many scientific calculators, which have 256 KB. Modern computers operate something like 60,000 times faster than the Apollo unit.

lunar module

NERVES OF STEEL

When Apollo 11's lunar module neared the Moon's surface, the computer overloaded and locked up. Neil Armstrong took the controls and landed the "Eagle" manually with seconds to spare.

MEMORY MATCH-UP

Apollo unit: 6 transistors

iPhone X: approx. 4.3 billion transistors

237

IN 1955, 5 MB OF DATA WEIGHED A LOT!

The world's first computer storage device—IBM's 305 RAMAC—was packed into a sleek cabinet the size of two refrigerators and required a forklift truck to lift—not quite laptop-ready! Its 50 bulky aluminum discs stored about 5 MB.

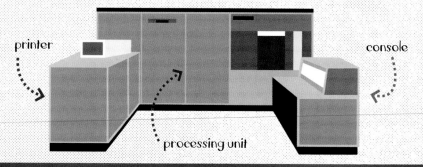

printer

console

processing unit

BITS 'N' BYTES

Bit—The smallest unit of data.
It can be either a 0 or a 1.

Byte—1 byte = 8 bits

Terabyte
1 TB = 1,000,000,000,000,000 bytes
10 TB is all the books in the Library of Congress

Yottabyte
1 YB = 1,000,000,000,000,000,000,000,000 bytes
The Internet holds about a yottabyte of data

2 terabytes of photos are uploaded to social media websites every day.

THE WORLD'S FIRST WEBSITE
WAS BUILT IN 1990

Welcome to the weird, wonderful, and wacky Web.

TOTALLY TANGLED TECHNOLOGY

The **World Wide Web (WWW)** is a platform that sits on top of the Internet. Each of its pages has an address, called a **URL** (Universal Resource Locator), so that it can be accessed by the Internet. Web pages are linked to each other via hyperlinks. A collection of linked web pages is a website.

Visit the world's first web page (it's still there) at:
http://info.cern.ch/hypertext/WWW/TheProject.html
(But don't hold your breath—historic it may be, but it's no thriller!)

The NeXT machine that was the original web server is still at CERN, in Geneva, Switzerland.

THE WORLD'S MOST COMMON
PASSWORD IS 123456

NO PROTECTION

Nearly half the world uses easy-to-guess passwords to protect their computers, e-mail, and bank accounts. Poor passwords include strings of numbers or letters, such as "1111" or "qwerty," and proper words, such as "monkey." Even changing common letters to numbers, such "ch33se" is flimsy.

ABOUT 5,000 NEW COMPUTER VIRUSES ARE RELEASED EVERY MONTH

INFECTION STATION

Malware is a damaging computer code that makes its home in your PC. Once installed, the bogus software takes control and spreads to other computers. Here is a spotter's guide to types of malware to watch out for in the Internet jungle.

VIRUS
A program that inserts itself into apps and waits for the user to fire up the program.

BOTNETS
A zombie army of machines, remotely controlled without the users' permission.

WORMS
Stand-alone programs that spread copies across a computer network, gobbling processing power and bandwidth.

TROJAN HORSE
A program that pretends to be useful, but gives hackers a "backdoor" into your PC.

QUANTUM COMPUTERS ARE 100 MILLION TIMES FASTER . . .

. . . than your home PC. They will soon solve problems that would take normal supercomputers millions of years!

QUBITS

Quantum computers use qubits. A **qubit** (say cue-bit) is a "quantum bit." Unlike traditional computer bits, which store information as 0s and 1s, qubits can be set to 0, a 1, or both at the same time! This gives quantum computers a huge boost when it comes to number crunching.

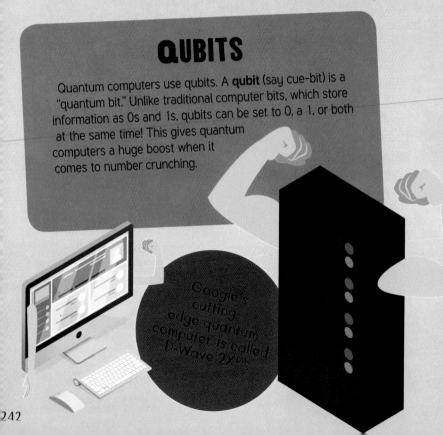

Google's cutting-edge quantum computer is called D-Wave 2X™.

THE @ SYMBOL IS THE NEWEST CHARACTER IN MORSE CODE

Before telephones, people tapped out messages using Morse code. Amateur radio hobbyists and some ships still use this old-fashioned communication method.

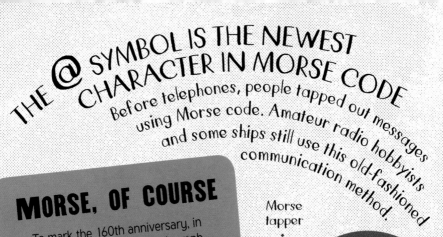

MORSE, OF COURSE

To mark the 160th anniversary, in 2004, of the first Morse telegraph transmission, the @ symbol was added to the official Morse code. It was the first new character added since World War I, and allows email addresses to be sent.

Morse tapper

The snail-like @ character is officially called the "commercial at" or "commat," but is usually known as the "at" sign.

Dot-dot-dash

Hello •••• • •–•• •–•• – – –

Be seeing you (BCNU) –•••• –•–• –• ••–

You are dotty •••– / •–• / –•• – – – – – – –•– –

243

RADICAL ROBOTS

Robot comes from a Czech word robota, which means hard work.

We already share our planet with 9 million robotic machines.

Robots assemble cars—and drive them—disarm bombs, deep-sea dive in Antarctic water, explore distant planets, . . . and vacuum carpets.

Robots can go into environments that would be dangerous for humans.

The first robot ever was a mechanical bird, built in 400 BCE, that flew 656 ft (200 m).

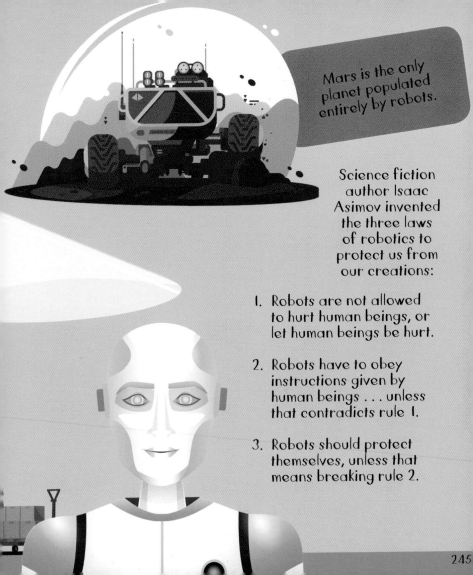

Mars is the only planet populated entirely by robots.

Science fiction author Isaac Asimov invented the three laws of robotics to protect us from our creations:

1. Robots are not allowed to hurt human beings, or let human beings be hurt.

2. Robots have to obey instructions given by human beings . . . unless that contradicts rule 1.

3. Robots should protect themselves, unless that means breaking rule 2.

245

NEW BODY PARTS
CAN BE GROWN IN THE LAB

Very soon surgeons will be able to replace your worn-out body parts, just as car mechanics repair cars.

BODY SHOP

Scientists are learning how to grow human body parts, from muscles, blood vessels, and skin, to hearts, bladders, ears, noses, and even brain tissue!

salamander

ANIMAL SUPERPOWERS

Starfish and salamanders have no problems regrowing missing arms and tails. Should they lose it, flatworms can even grow a new head.

How to grow a new ear:

1. 3D print a plastic "scaffold."

2. Seed the scaffold with stem cells and bathe them in a cell soup.

3. Marvel while new cells grow over it like a garden.

SPIDER-GOATS
ARE A REAL THING

OMG! GMO!

A **genetically modified organism** (GMO) is a living thing that carries DNA modified by genetic engineering. One example is frost-resistant tomatoes, which contain antifreeze genes from an Arctic fish. Although a GMO makes people think of mutants with weird powers, most are actually bug-resistant plants.

SPIDER-GOAT, SPIDER-GOAT

To make a supergoat that "spins" silk, scientists in 1999 inserted the silk-producing gene from a spider into the DNA of an ordinary goat. The milk of this spider-goat contains silk proteins, and lots of it. The proteins can be separated from the milk to produce an ultralight, mega-strong silk.

ALL BANANAS ARE CLONES

Cloning is the creation of identical copies of a cell or a whole living thing. A clone has exactly the same DNA as the original. Bananas and many other plants are clones, as are most bacteria. Identical twins are clones, too.

HOW TO CLONE A SHEEP

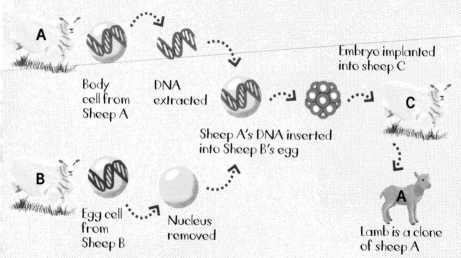

A

Body cell from Sheep A

DNA extracted

Sheep A's DNA inserted into Sheep B's egg

Embryo implanted into sheep C

C

B

Egg cell from Sheep B

Nucleus removed

A

Lamb is a clone of sheep A

SEND IN THE CLONES!

The most famous type of cloning is **reproductive cloning**. In 1996, this process made Dolly the sheep the first cloned animal. Human cloning is illegal in most countries.

THE MOST EXPENSIVE MEAT PATTY
COST $331,400

WHAT'S YOUR BEEF?

In 2013, two volunteers sat down in front of an audience in London to eat a burger. The strange show was a public tasting of artificially produced beef. The small slab of lab-made meat had taken three months to grow at a cost of $331,400.

COLD SHOULDER

Artificial meat, also known as "schmeat," is made from stem cells taken from a cow's shoulder. In the lab it is grown into long strips of muscles. Fans say that it not only saves animals' lives, but also protects the environment. Critics say it's weird and tastes strange!

JUST 473 GENES
ARE NECESSARY FOR LIFE

LIFE 2.0

Genes are short "clips" of DNA held on long coiled strands called **chromosomes**. They contain the coded instructions to keep the body running. Many genes do the same job, however. Scientist Craig Venter and his team snipped out genes one by one from a bacterial cell, keeping only the essential ones. They ended up with a fully functioning microbe with just 473 genes—the smallest genome of any single-celled living organism.

Free-living bacteria normally have around 1,500–7,500 genes.

gene

GENE GENIUS

A genome is the complete set of DNA in a cell.

MUTANT MOSQUITOES MAY DEFEAT MALARIA

SWAMP SICKNESS

Malaria is a tropical disease spread by mosquito bites. It makes red blood cells explode, giving people fevers and chills.

Malaria kills over half a million people every year.

INSECT CONTROL

Scientists are breeding mosquitoes with a gene that makes the female unable to reproduce. If released into the wild, this could reduce the number of mosquitoes and the spread of malaria. However, scientists don't know if wild mosquitoes will become resistant, or if removing mosquitoes from the ecosystem will create new problems.

EVERY MAGNET HAS A NORTH POLE AND A SOUTH POLE

MYSTERIOUS MAGNETS

Split a bar magnet in two, and you don't get separate north and south poles. Instead, you get two new magnets, each with a north and south end—a **dipole**. Even if you go right down to single particles, you still end up with a magnetic dipole.

NORTH OR SOUTH?

MONOPOLY

Theoretically, a single magnetic pole—called a **monopole**—can exist. But no one has detected one yet.

Poles apart?

Earth's North Pole is actually a south pole. The north pole of a compass magnet is attracted to a magnetic south pole, which is in the geographic North. Confusing!

MRI MAGNETS ARE STRONG ENOUGH TO TEAR A WATCH OFF YOUR ARM

SUPER-COOL ELECTROMAGNETS

Electromagnets, such as those found in MRI machines, are coils of wire wrapped around a metal bar. They use electricity to create a magnetic field, and can be switched on and off. The most powerful electromagnets are large, and must be kept cool to work.

Feel the force

An **MRI** uses magnetic fields and radio waves to produce a detailed image of soft tissue and bone. The pull of an MRI machine's magnets is so strong, you must remove any metal in your pockets. The doctors also need to know if you have metal objects, such as plates, pacemakers, or piercings, in your body.

An MRI's maximum magnetic forcefield is 4,000 times stronger than Earth's magnetic field.

ELECTRIC FIELDS
CAN BEND A FLAME

You can shape fire with electricity!

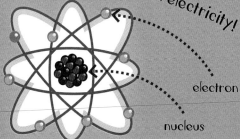

electron

nucleus

flattened flame

FIRE POWER

If you put a flame between positively and negatively charged metal plates, the flame will reach toward the negative one. Why is that? Air is made up of atoms. In every one of those atoms, negatively charged electrons whiz around a positively charged nucleus. Heat from a candle flame can force the electrons from air molecules to fly off, leaving positively charged atoms called **ions**. The ions are pulled toward the negatively charged plate, changing the shape of the flame.

THE LARGE HADRON COLLIDER IS THE WORLD'S BIGGEST MACHINE

The LHC is a ring-shaped particle accelerator that is changing our understanding of the Universe.

Smashing science

Tiny particles of matter zoom around a tunnel on the French–Swiss border. Protons can do the 16.7-mile (27-km) loop 11,245 times per second–that's very close to the speed of light itself. When they smash together–"BOOM!"–a blinding flash of energy gives us a glimpse of what happened to matter shortly after the Big Bang.

Super-duper discovery

After smashing particles together, the LHC searches the "crash site" for unusual types of matter. In 2012, scientists discovered the **Higgs boson particle**, which is thought to give mass to matter.

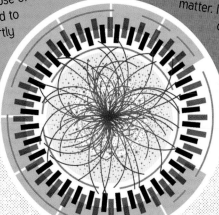

GRAVITY IS THE WEAKEST FUNDAMENTAL FORCE

DOWN TO EARTH

Gravity is the force that keeps our feet on the ground and holds the planets in orbit around the Sun. It certainly doesn't feel weak when you fall down. However, the gravitational pull of the whole planet on an iron nail can be easily beaten by a small bar magnet.

Gravity is 10 thousand trillion trillion trillion times weaker than the electromagnetic force.

FUNDAMENTAL FORCES

Just four interactions keep our Universe ticking. The **strong force** and the **weak force** hold together the nucleus in atoms. **Electromagnetism** has to do with electricity, magnetism, and the way atoms interact. **Gravity** draws objects with mass together.

Electrons in a wire
MOVE AT THE SPEED OF SPREADING HONEY

Flick on the radio and it squawks to life immediately.

LIGHTNING SPEED

An **electric current** is made by electrons moving in a wire. Although individual electrons move sluggishly, the electromagnetic wave that ripples through the wire travels close to the speed of light—around 167,770 miles (270,000 km) per second! This pulse makes all the electrons start moving at almost the same instant.

Electrons in a wire move about 0.04 in (1 mm) per second.

257

INVISIBLE RAYS

Our eyes can sense some types of electromagnetic radiation. We call those types **visible light**.

There are other types of electromagnetic radiation that we can't see.

Microwave radiation is used for cell phone networks and to quickly cook food.

Radio waves are mostly used for TV, radio, and telephone communication.

Radio waves can travel around the world and be bounced off satellites in space.

Radio telescopes pick up weak radio waves arriving from outer space.

night-vision goggles

Hot things give off light, too. This infrared radiation is picked up by night-vision goggles.

Penetrating **X-rays** are used to look inside the body, because they travel through muscle, but not bone.

Released by nuclear reactors and bombs, **gamma rays** are the most energetic form of light.

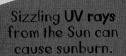

Sizzling **UV rays** from the Sun can cause sunburn.

259

If we could see microwaves
THE SKY WOULD BE ABLAZE

COSMIC GLOW

One of the most important discoveries ever was made in 1964—totally by accident. Two scientists trying to get rid of the static noise in their satellite receiver found that the whole sky was lit by a faint glow coming from all directions. This is called the **cosmic microwave background (CMB)**.

BABY PHOTO OF THE UNIVERSE

The CMB is the oldest light that we can see. Produced at the moment that light was first released into the early Universe, it is what is left of the firestorm of energy that created our Universe.

MICROWAVES WERE DISCOVERED BY ACCIDENT

RAPID HEATING

Useful for defrosting food and making popcorn, the microwave oven is an essential part of a modern kitchen. The appliance was invented in 1946, when engineer Percy Spencer stood next to a magnetron (a microwave-producing tube) and the chocolate bar in his pocket turned into a gooey, sticky mess. Curious, he popped an egg under the device. It exploded, splattering his face with egg.

HOT WATER

Microwaves work by transferring energy to water molecules in the food. As they vibrate more, the food heats up.

STRANGE BUT TRUE

Your Internet router also sends out microwaves, but it won't cook you!

WHEN YOU FALL, THERE'S A
SPEED LIMIT

SKY'S THE LIMIT

Terminal velocity is the maximum speed at which anything can fall. Jump out of an aircraft and, in theory, you continue picking up speed as you plunge to Earth. In reality, however, the air in the atmosphere resists your movement. At a certain point, air resistance becomes greater than gravity and you slow down, until the forces are balanced. Falling belly down and lying flat like a plank, you can reach a terminal velocity of around 120 mph (200 kph).

FASTEST FALL

Daredevil Felix Baumgartner hit 843.6 mph (1,357.64 kph) during his 2012 skydive from space.

A BUTTERFLY FLAPPING ITS WINGS IN BRAZIL CAN CAUSE A TORNADO IN THE USA

THE BUTTERFLY EFFECT

Scientists use powerful supercomputers to predict outcomes in real-world systems, such as the weather. The computers are fed data about the system and use it to make a prediction about what might happen in the future. Obviously, the more data reported, the better the prediction. However, for complex systems, unimportant changes—such as the tiny air currents made by a butterfly flapping its wings—can have large, unexpected effects.

CHAOS REIGNS

There is no way of measuring every single thing in a complex system. This is why we can't predict weather more than a few days in advance.

100 BILLION NEUTRINOS PASS THROUGH YOU EVERY SECOND

"Neutrino" means "little neutral one."

neutrino

GHOST PARTICLES

A **neutrino** is one of the hardest particles to detect. Neutrinos weigh next to nothing, carry no electrical charge, and travel at nearly the speed of light. Because neutrinos are so tiny, and unmoved by magnetic and electric fields, solid substances are mostly empty space to them. They zip straight through the 7,918-mile (12,742-km)–wide Earth as if it wasn't there.

Most of the neutrinos that whiz through your body come from the Sun.

No one is sure why the
UNIVERSE IS MOSTLY MATTER

Matter has an evil twin, called **antimatter**.

matter atom

antimatter atom

KEY

●	+	proton
●	O	neutron
●	−	electron
●	−	antiproton
●	O	antineutron
●	+	positron

DOUBLE TROUBLE

Each particle of matter has a matching anti-self. With an equal mass, an antimatter particle looks the same as its normal matter twin. However, it has opposite charge and reversed "spin."* When matter meets its anti-self, both blow up and destroy each other, leaving nothing behind.

MYSTERY MATTER

Super-energetic explosions in science labs create matter and antimatter in equal amounts. If this had happened during the Big Bang, the matter and antimatter would have completely wiped each other out. So why didn't this happen? Nobody knows!

*Charge and spin are basic properties of subatomic particles.

DISEASE ISN'T SPREAD
BY INVISIBLE GASES

UNSEEN BADDIES

Today we know that diseases are spread by microscopic organisms. However, it was once a controversial idea! Doctors and scientists used to think that sickness was caused by poisonous gases. What changed that? Well, you need a microscope to see germs. Germ theory is crucial to modern ideas about hygiene. Now, wash your hands!

COVER YOUR FACE

Sneezes spread thousands of tiny droplets of mucus and saliva, loaded with germs, into the air. Most of the time, your body fights off germs, but when your resistance is low you can get an infection.

THE MYSTERIOUS PLACEBO EFFECT
MAKES US BETTER WITHOUT MEDICINE

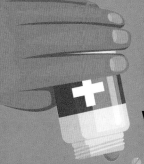

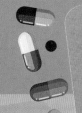

MEDICINES FOR DUMMIES

Fake drugs can make people feel better. A **placebo** is a dummy medicine containing nothing more effective than sugar. However, if someone thinks they are receiving treatment, their symptoms can actually improve. Medical experts are amazed by the way the human mind turns something fake into something that actually works!

TESTING TIMES

In blind trials of a new drug, half the test subjects receive the real drug and half get a placebo. The outcomes of both groups are compared to see if the treatment performs better than a dud sugar pill.

THE LOWEST POSSIBLE TEMPERATURE IS -273.15 °C

FROZEN SOLID

Scientists have a special temperature scale for measuring the heat energy in substances. It is called the **Kelvin scale**, named after the Scottish physicist William Thompson (aka Lord Kelvin). Zero Kelvin is the lower limit of cold. Called "**absolute zero**," it is the temperature at which atoms stop dead and there is no heat energy left.

ROCK BOTTOM

Absolute zero is actually impossible to reach. That's because no matter how chilly it gets, there is always some energy due to the wiggling of particles at the smallest, "quantum" level. This quantum movement is what keeps helium liquid right down to the very coldest temperatures.

boiling point of water

human body temperature

room temperature

freezing point of water

absolute zero

A PERFECT VACUUM IS IMPOSSIBLE

Outer space contains fewer than one molecule per 35 ft³ (1 m³).

EXTREME VACUUM

The purest vacuum ever would have no matter in it whatsoever. But even the best vacuum pumps leave the odd particle inside a container. Fingerprint smudges, plastics, and certain metals on the airlocks or walls give off vapor in high-vacuum conditions.

EMPTY SPACE

The most complete vacuum is in outer space. That is why astronauts wear special pressure suits and carry their own oxygen supply to breathe. However, even space contains tiny particles of cosmic dust floating around, along with atoms of hydrogen and helium.

SOUND WAVES

The loudest sound ever recorded was the eruption of Krakatoa volcano in 1883.

The quietest place on Earth is an echo-free chamber in Minnesota, absorbing 99.99% of sound.

The tremendous crack destroyed the tiny Indonesian island and echoed four times around the planet.

It's true: in space no one can hear you scream. Sound energy travels by vibrating particles. Space is empty.

People with "misophonia" hate certain noises such as eating, lip-smacking, pen-clicking, tapping, and typing.

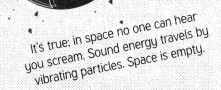

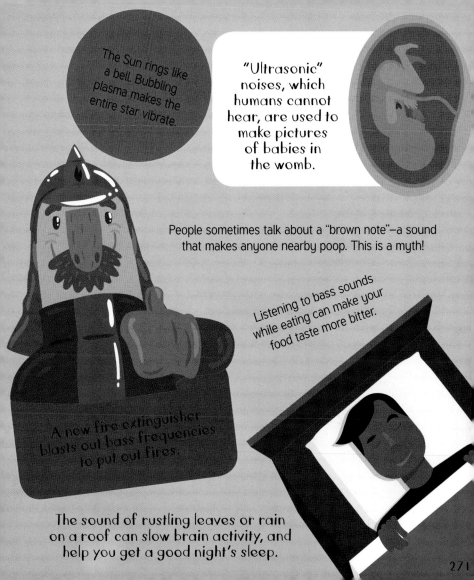

The Sun rings like a bell. Bubbling plasma makes the entire star vibrate.

"Ultrasonic" noises, which humans cannot hear, are used to make pictures of babies in the womb.

People sometimes talk about a "brown note"–a sound that makes anyone nearby poop. This is a myth!

Listening to bass sounds while eating can make your food taste more bitter.

A new fire extinguisher blasts out bass frequencies to put out fires.

The sound of rustling leaves or rain on a roof can slow brain activity, and help you get a good night's sleep.

271

WIND NEVER BLOWS IN STRAIGHT LINES

SWIRLING STORMS

Wind is just the movement of air caused by differences in pressure in the atmosphere. Wind blows from places with a high pressure to lower pressure areas. However, because the planet is spinning, wind travels in curves. This is called the **Coriolis effect**, and it explains why tropical storms swirl clockwise in the northern hemisphere and anticlockwise in the southern hemisphere.

You have 1.1 tons (1 tonne) of air pressing down on you—that's the weight of a small car.

INVISIBLE FORCES ACT ON BODIES IN MOTION

Forces can't be seen and some can make objects move without even touching them. These strange powers that govern how objects move were first described by super-scientist Isaac Newton.

THREE LAWS OF MOTION:

1 Things stay put, or keep moving at a constant speed, unless a force acts on them. (It doesn't require constant force to keep things moving.*)

2 Forces make things change speed.

3 For every force applied, there is an equal force in the opposite direction.

forces in play

*So long as there are no forces resisting movement. Friction resists movement, which is why riding a bike does require constant force.

rule 3 in action (and reaction!)

THE SECRET SHAPE OF WINGS MAKES PLANES FLY

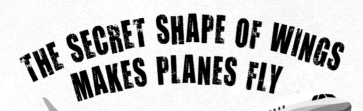

WING'S THE THING

When you climb into a metal tube and zoom off into the sky, it's comforting to know that physics can explain what keeps you up there. Planes' wings are shaped in a way that makes air move faster over the top than underneath the wing. That creates lift.

3. Higher pressure under the wing generates an upward, lifting force.

Lift force

1. Air moving over the top of a wing moves quickly and has low pressure.

2. Air coming off the trailing edge of the wing is thrown down. This also generates an upward force.

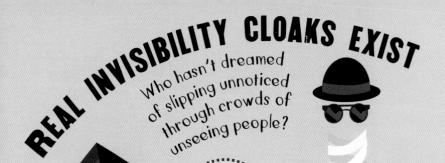

REAL INVISIBILITY CLOAKS EXIST

Who hasn't dreamed of slipping unnoticed through crowds of unseeing people?

stealth plane

GOING STEALTH

Hiding in plain sight usually involves thwarting detection technology. **Stealth planes** have a cunning radar-baffling shape, quiet internal wing-engines, and radar-absorbing paint. However, they still cast shadows.

CLOAKING DEVICE

Scientists are working with magical-sounding metamaterials. While not yet as good as Harry Potter's invisibility cloak, these divert light rays around them, making it look as if they are not there. Since the light path around an object is longer than one that travels directly through that space, they are still detectable.

SMOKE PARTICLES REVEAL
INVISIBLE ATOMS AND MOLECULES

WIGGLY JIGGLY

Stick some smoke particles, dust motes, or pollen grains in water under a microscope and you'll see they do a jittery dance, careering all over the place. Scottish scientist Robert Brown discovered this **Brownian motion** in 1827.

LET ME ATOM!

In 1905, über-brain Albert Einstein thought that this random motion might be caused by invisible atoms of gas (or water molecules) colliding with larger smoke or pollen grains. He crunched the numbers and proved mathematically that matter is made of tiny particles, and could even cleverly predict how big atoms are.

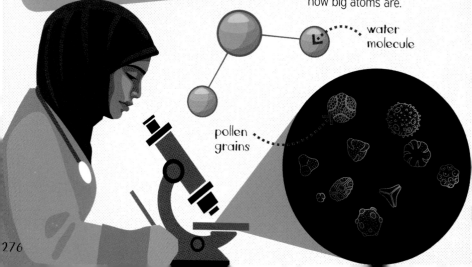

water molecule

pollen grains

A DUTCH CLOTH MERCHANT WAS THE FIRST TO SEE MICROBES

microsopic creatures

LITTLE CREATURES

In the 1670s, Antonie van Leeuwenhoek was the first person to gaze upon a hidden world. Leeuwenhoek (say Lay-ven-hook) made the best magnifying glasses in the world, which he used to check the quality of cloth. But when he looked at dirty pond water, he could see wriggling beasts smaller than anything else anyone had ever seen.

BACTERIAL PLANET

Humans are not typical organisms. Most living things on Earth are tiny single-celled organisms you need to use a microscope to see.

There are more microbugs in a pinch of soil than people on the planet.

WE ONLY EVER SEE
ONE SIDE OF THE MOON

STUCK ON YOU

The Moon isn't stuck in place with one side facing us. If it wasn't spinning, we'd see all sides of it as it moves around the planet. Instead, the Moon spins exactly once on its axis every time it orbits Earth, so it always keeps the same side toward us.

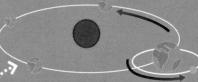

Earth orbits the Sun

Moon orbits Earth

PERFECT SYNC

This is called **tidal locking**. Earth's larger gravity has acted like a brake and slowed the spin of its smaller companion.

OVER THE MOON

The first time humans got to see the "far side" of the Moon was in 1959, thanks to the Soviet spacecraft Luna 3.

STARS ARE STILL THERE IN THE DAY

Stars and galaxies don't disappear in the day! They are invisible because the light from our own star is so bright.

starless sky

BLINDED BY THE LIGHT

During the night, we face away from the Sun and the marvels of space are revealed. But as the Earth swings us back around, the radiation streaming off our star makes the sky glow blue and blinds us to the faint light from the stars.

starry night

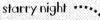

GOOD MORNING, MOON

The Moon is bright enough to be visible in the daytime. Unless there is a new moon, you can see it nearly every day.

LIGHT IS BOTH A PARTICLE AND A WAVE

Different experiments show light as "blips" or "ripples."

IT'S A WAVE!

Visible light is the type of electromagnetic radiation that humans can see. It ripples through electric and magnetic fields and, unlike a sound wave or a wave moving through water, it doesn't need "stuff" to travel through. Because it can cross the empty vacuum of space, we can see light from the stars.

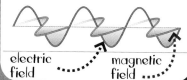

LIGHT, MOVING AS A RIPPLE

electric field   magnetic field

IT'S A PARTICLE!

Other experiments show that light comes in packages or blips called **photons**. Photons fly through space like tiny bullets.

So, is light a wave or a particle? Amazingly, it is both!

THE QUANTUM WORLD IS WEIRD

At the smallest scale, the rules are very different.

STRANGER THINGS

Scientists exploring the world at a quantum scale—smaller even than atoms—have found a place with very different rules. Quantum particles can only have fixed amounts of energy, and "click" between them with no in-between amounts, a bit like gears on a bike. In the normal-sized world, however, you don't notice the tiny quantum effects.

photons

QUANTUM ENERGY

When light interacts with subatomic particles, it is "chunked." Each packet of light—or photon—carries a fixed amount of energy.

QUANTUM WEIRDNESS

The rules of the Universe are very different in the quantum realm!

Particles can get paired with each other, so that what happens to one will affect the other.

This "quantum entanglement" works, even if the particles are at opposite ends of the Universe.

It's impossible to know where a particle is and know its speed at the same time.

One of the spookiest quantum effects is that particles can be in two places at the same time.

Quantum effects keep life on Earth going—without them, the Sun would stop shining and plants would not be able to take energy from sunlight.

Quantum tunneling is where particles appear on the other side of a barrier without moving over or through it.

European robins have a magnetic sense. Experiments have shown that it uses quantum effects!

Sounds like magic? Quantum tunneling is how the microchip switches in electronic devices work.

In 2017, Chinese scientists used quantum entanglement to teleport photons from the surface of Earth into space.

THERE MIGHT BE OTHER "YOU"S IN PARALLEL UNIVERSES

Your mind. Officially blown.

PARALLEL UNIVERSES?

As well as the one you live in, there may be* many alternate Universes.

LIKE HOW MANY?

Infinitely many. If the theories are true** there are countless other worlds.

SO, FORGET "UNIVERSE?"

Yeah. "Uni" means one. We've got us a "multiverse," baby!

WHY ARE THERE MULTIPLE "ME"S?

Because there are infinite worlds, there are countless Earths and countless "you"s. Every conceivable possibility happens—in one you're at the top of the heap, in the other, you're at the very bottom.

*In theory!

**We have no way of proving this ... yet

84

GAMMA–RAY BURSTS ARE THE UNIVERSE'S BIGGEST EXPLOSIONS

Satellites launched in the 1960s made an unexpected discovery.

FLASHY STUFF

Gamma-ray bursts (GRBs) are flashes of ultra-high energy radiation coming from outer space. Lasting as little as a few milliseconds, they capture the moment a massive star dies. They are the brightest and most powerful bangs in the Universe.

GRBs shine a million times brighter than an entire galaxy!

COSMIC RAYS

THINGS GET HEAVIER THE FASTER THEY TRAVEL

The Universe has a speed limit . . .

If things could travel faster, reality would be in trouble— an arrow might hit its target before a bow was fired!

DO NOT EXCEED 186,282 MILES PER SECOND (299,792 KM PER SECOND)

The most famous equation in science . . .

$$E = mc^2$$

. . . says that mass and energy are the same thing. Since light has no mass, it zips along at max speed. Particles of matter, however, need energy to make them go faster, and so gain extra mass. This means they need more and more energy until finally, there isn't enough energy in the Universe to push them to the speed of light.

TIME IS SLOWER FOR PEOPLE WHO TRAVEL VERY FAST

Time isn't the same for everyone.

CLOCK WATCHING

Time does funny things around the speed of light. Imagine a pair of twins. One stays on Earth, while the other one travels at near-lightspeed to a nearby star. On his return, the spacefaring twin would be younger than his stay-at-home sibling. Why? Time would have slowed down on the high-speed trip, meaning that fewer years would have passed for that twin.

Albert Einstein

This **Twin Paradox** was one of the strange predictions made by Einstein's theory of relativity.

NOTHING ESCAPES A BLACK HOLE

Don't fall into a black hole! Its super-strong gravity would stretch you into spaghetti in an instant!

HOLES IN SPACE

No one has ever seen a black hole. That's because no light comes out of it, so it can't be seen. Black holes have so much matter squeezed inside them, they have stupendously strong gravity.

NO ESCAPE

To escape Earth's gravitational pull, an object must travel 6.8 miles/sec (11 kps)—about 33 times the speed of sound. That's an engineering problem. But the escape velocity from a black hole's gravity is greater than the speed of light. That's physically impossible for anything in our Universe.

GRAVITY MIGHT NOT EXIST

WEAK FORCE

Isaac Newton developed a theory about gravity in the 17th century, making it the fundamental force we've known about for longest. However, gravity is the least well-understood. We struggle to explain why it can only pull and not push, and we wonder why it is so weak and won't fit with quantum physics.

REBEL SCIENCE

A few brave scientists think that gravity might be a bit like temperature. We feel heat, but no individual particle has "heat." Instead, it arises out of the movement of microscopic particles. What if gravity is not a fundamental force at all, but something that arises from the way particles interact?

gravity at work

Sir Isaac Newton

A MYSTERIOUS DARK ENERGY IS PULLING THE UNIVERSE APART

Dark energy is the single biggest unsolved problem in science.

FAST FORWARD!

Our Universe is getting bigger. Instead of being slowed by the gravity of all the billions and trillions of stars it contains, its expansion is speeding up! Some mystery energy is defeating the force of gravity and astronomers can't explain it. That is why they call it "dark" energy.

DARK FORCE

Calculating the energy that is needed to defeat gravity, we find that dark energy must make up 70 percent of everything. It's hard to believe, but we are completely in the dark about three-quarters of our Universe!

MUCH OF THE UNIVERSE IS OUT OF REACH

HOW BIG IS THE Universe?

Unimaginably big, that's all you really need to know!

OBSERVABLE UNIVERSE

The part that we can see today extends about 14 billion light years in every direction. That forms an unimaginably massive sphere 28 billion light years across. But that is not all there is.

LOSING SIGHT OF THINGS

We can only see as far as light has journeyed over the Universe's lifetime. Space has expanded faster, however, whisking lots of the cosmos away and out of view.

observatory

EVEN BIGGER

It might be vast, but the Universe might be much, much bigger than what we can observe.

WAYS THE WORLD COULD END

The Planetary Defense Coordination Office (PDCO) in Washington D.C., USA, keeps the world safe from impacts from outer space.

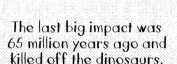

There are 1,489 potentially hazardous asteroids, bigger than 328 ft (100 m) across, that may come very close to Earth.

The PDCO monitors asteroids and comets whose orbits will bring them within 4.9 million miles (8 million km) of Earth.

The last big impact was 65 million years ago and killed off the dinosaurs.

An asteroid up to 6.2 miles (10 km) wide smashes into Earth about once every 100 million years.

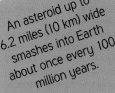

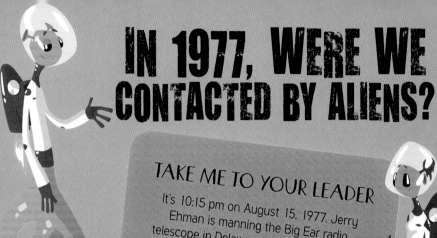

IN 1977, WERE WE CONTACTED BY ALIENS?

TAKE ME TO YOUR LEADER

It's 10:15 pm on August 15, 1977. Jerry Ehman is manning the Big Ear radio telescope in Delaware, Ohio. Suddenly, the equipment crackles with a pulse of radio waves coming out of the constellation of Sagittarius. It is 30 times more powerful than the background noise. Excitedly, he scribbles "Wow!" across the computer printout.

WOWSERS!

The 72-second "Wow!" signal has never happened again, and some people are SURE that this was contact with real-life aliens. In 2012, the Arecibo radio telescope in Puerto Rico beamed back a reply. The big "Hello from Earth" contained 10,000 Twitter messages, plus videos from celebrities.

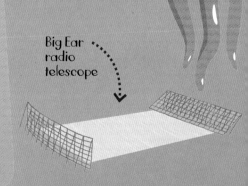

Big Ear radio telescope

THERE COULD BE 40 BILLION PLANETS
SIMILAR TO EARTH
ORBITING DISTANT SUNS

Too hot!

GOLDILOCKS ZONE

There are countless places that life might be hiding in the galaxy, but it makes sense to look for other planets like Earth. Because scientists think that liquid water is essential for life, they concentrate their search on "Goldilocks" planets—those planets that are "not too hot, not too cold, but just right," for water.

Too cold!

Just right!

PLANET HUNTING

NASA's Kepler space probe stares at distant stars, trying to spot a planet. It looks for shadows cast by planets as they cross the face of the star. Wobbles in starlight also help to detect invisible planets.

Kepler has spotted about 4,500 possible Earth-like planets.

THE SHAPES OF CRYSTALS FOLLOW INVISIBLE BLUEPRINTS OF ATOMS

The world's largest crystals are 36 ft (11 m) long—that's the same as 58 pencils laid end-to-end.

ORDER FROM DISORDER

Crystals are beautiful natural solids. The atoms inside a crystal are invisible. They may not show how they are organized, but they leave some pretty big hints on the surface. Their flat faces, sharp edges, and angles all reflect their orderly internal arrangement.

X-RAY SPECS

To see the invisible internal arrangements of atoms, we fire invisible X-rays at them. These rays bounce off the atoms and the reflections reveal their hidden structure.

Invasion of the body snatchers

Viruses are out for themselves. They spread by hijacking living cells and turning them into zombie virus factories. The cell ignores warning signals and keeps pumping out copies of the invader. This ends badly for the cell. Ripped open, it dies, releasing many new viruses to infect other cells. Fighting viral infections is what makes people feel ill. The common cold, flu, chicken pox, and measles are all illnesses caused by viruses.

The body does have ways of fighting back against viruses.

1. One type of white blood cell surrounds viruses.

2. It engulfs them and breaks them down.

3. Other white blood cells make antibodies.

4. Antibodies are designed to detect specific viruses.

5. Once they find the viruses, they destroy them.

NO ONE HAS EVER SEEN A THOUGHT

Scientists are only just beginning to reveal the mysteries of the brain.

MIND READING

For most of history, scientists could only look at the brains of dead people (or use damaged brains to figure out which parts did what). Now, thanks to CT and MRI scans, they can watch a living brain thinking. However, not even our most advanced machines can show us our own thoughts. MRI machines can, however, trace brain activity. We can watch the amazing sight of individual brain cells firing, but we can't read each other's minds.

Brain cells firing

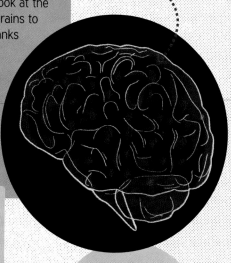

The human brain is the most complex known structure in the Universe.

AIR POLLUTION IS A DEADLY, INVISIBLE KILLER

Invisible toxic particles in the air are poisoning our cities.

TOXIC TRAFFIC

Air pollution is made of poisonous gases, and fine, almost-invisible particles of soot, dust, and chemicals. These come from the exhaust gases of road traffic, power stations, factories, fires, and chemical and paint spraying. Breathing them in air is harmful to the lungs over a long period, particularly for children.

CITY SICKNESS

Nitrogen dioxide is a brown gas. This waste product of burning fossil fuels causes breathing difficulties. It mainly comes from cars and trucks.

Some cities are banning diesel vehicles because they cause more pollution than other types of vehicles.

IT'S HARD TO EXPLAIN
WHAT ENERGY IS...
You cannot see energy. You cannot hold it. So . . .

. . . WHAT IS ENERGY?

Energy is the stuff that makes things happen. You can observe its effects—food makes people go. The faster the moving thing, the bigger the smash. Energy doesn't exist on its own; instead, it is always carried by something.

Energy is nothing more than a (very) useful idea. This one:

Energy is the ability to do work.*

One of the most basic laws of physics is that energy can't be created or destroyed.

*Work means moving something against a force.

...BUT WE CAN EXPLAIN WHY YOUR
BEDROOM IS A MESS!

ENERGY ENIGMA

The Universe is only here because of energy. It can't be created or destroyed ... but what happens to it over time? The answer is **entropy**.

WHAT IS ENTROPY?

There are loads of different kinds of energy, and it happily swaps from one kind to another. However, you can't stop energy spreading out. This is why coffee gets cold and why smells spread.

LOVE CHAOS

The same spreading out thing happens with your bedroom. Because there are many more ways in which your room can be messy than tidy, messy is much more likely. Explain that to your folks—"it's not me, it's entropy!"

INDEX

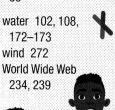